The Beautiful Sermon

Image and the Aesthetics of Preaching

DEAN NADASDY

CONCORDIA SEMINARY PRESS
Saint Louis

The Beautiful Sermon: Image and the Aesthetics of Preaching

PUBLISHED BY CONCORDIA SEMINARY PRESS

Concordia Seminary
801 Seminary Place
St. Louis, Missouri 63105

ISBN 978-0-911770-84-1

Library of Congress Control Number: 2021944099

ABOUT THE COVER: **Rembrandt Harmensz van Rijn,**
Christ Preaching (La Petite Tombe), ca. 1652, Rijksmuseum, Amsterdam, The Netherlands

Book layout & design: P.Berkbigler Design & Multimedia, LLC.

To Susie
Beauty is as beauty does.

The Beautiful Sermon

Image and the Aesthetics of Preaching

CONTENTS

FOREWORD: *CONVERSATIONS IN PREACHING*

To preach is to enter a holy conversation. This conversation has been going on long before we came to the table and will continue long after we have shared our thoughts, thanked our host, and gone home.

Principally, the conversation is between God and his people. After all, preaching is the living voice of God who, in Jesus Christ, graciously speaks his people into life. This conversation, however, also includes the insights of theologians, the guidance of pastors, and the performance of preachers, past and present. It is deep enough to dialog with God's people, drawing wisdom from the mutual consolation of the saints, and it is broad enough to embrace the voices of culture, as Paul so richly showed in the Court of the Areopagus. These varied voices stimulate thought. They raise questions we didn't know we were asking, evoke answers we didn't know we had, and provoke reflection on timely truths that need to be timely spoken. Such is the shape, the give and take, of our table talk when we enter conversations in preaching.

The Conversations in Preaching series is an opportunity for Lutheran preachers to reflect on the heart and the art of preaching. Unfortunately, one of the difficulties of being a preacher is that one rarely has time to read and reflect on the practice. After all, one is too busy preaching. This series has been written for such active preachers.

Each book in the series will take up one topic relevant to the preaching task and begin a conversation. The conversation is not meant to be comprehensive (covering all that has been written or taught about the topic) nor definitive (offering the only way one can respond to the topic), but rather exploratory, giving readers a chance to reflect with a preacher, theoretically, theologically, and practically, about one aspect of preaching.

At the heart of the conversation will be a Lutheran sensibility of preaching. Preaching is the authoritative public proclamation of the faith, normed and guided by the Scriptures, centered in the gospel of Jesus Christ for forgiveness, life, and salvation, for the benefit of the hearers in their relationship to God and to others. But the art of the conversation will be how that sensibility relates to other issues. It could be a current trend in homiletical theory or an ancient form of homiletical practice.

Each book highlights one topic for conversation and the format invites preachers to reflect on their practice and grow in their preaching. In the opening chapter, the writer will introduce the topic and situate it within current homiletical theory. Then, in the chapters that follow, the author will unfold the Lutheran contribution to the conversation. Finally, each book will close with sample sermons and commentary that demonstrate what the theory looks like in practice.

Our prayer is that these books will aid your growth in preaching. With them, we invite you to take a seat at the table around God's word. Here you will be fed and led into conversation so that, ultimately, you rise and go to speak to others of what our Lord has done.

With that understanding, I invite you to consider the aesthetics of preaching by reading and listening to the work of the Rev. Dr. Dean Nadasdy. Dr. Nadasdy was the first occupant of the Gregg H. Benidt Endowed Memorial Chair in Homiletics and Literature at Concordia Seminary, St. Louis (1997–2000), where he served as associate professor of practical theology. He has also served as pastor of Woodbury Lutheran Church, Woodbury, MN (2000–2012), Cross View Lutheran Church, Edina, MN (1981–1997), and Grace Lutheran Church, Eugene, OR (1973–1981), and most recently as president of the Minnesota South District of The Lutheran Church—Missouri Synod (2012–2018). His experience integrating the arts and congregational life, his dramatic works (*Cross Views: Story Dramas That Teach the Faith and Gospel Dramas*), and his years of faithful preaching, all give him a wonderful voice to begin our conversation on the integration of preaching and the arts.

David R. Schmitt
Gregg H. Benidt Memorial Professor of Homiletics and Literature,
Concordia Seminary, St. Louis

The Conversations in Preaching series is made possible by the generous support of The J. Ernest and Elsie Schneider Endowment for Excellence in Relevant Preaching at Concordia Seminary, St. Louis.

PREFACE

My thanks to David Schmitt and Travis Scholl who suggested this project in connection with the dedication of commissioned stained-glass windows for the Chapel of St. Timothy and St. Titus at Concordia Seminary, St. Louis. In that beautiful setting for worship, no doubt, beautiful sermons will continue to be preached—theirs among them. I thank David Schmitt as well for his helpful suggestions in preparing the manuscript and for his foreword to this book.

Along the way of writing this little book, I was often reminded of my time at Concordia Seminary as a homiletics student of Dr. Richard ("Doc") Caemmerer. I recall being transfixed by his preaching in chapel services. I remember Caemmerer often preaching with his eyes shut, as if seeing in his imagination what he was preaching. It was then, in his chapel sermons, that I first began to recognize the beauty attendant to preaching.

Brought to mind as well by this project were my own homiletics students at Concordia Seminary when I held the Benidt Chair in Homiletics and Literature and later taught as a guest instructor. Recurring mental portraits of former students came to mind, especially those who were in the DMin course in homiletics over the last twenty years. As one would expect, some of the sermons I've read and heard have been more beautiful than others. What lingers, though, is the commitment of preachers across generations to grow in their preaching skills. That commitment itself brings a beauty to the preaching task and hope for more beautiful sermons.

Finally, I recall with gratitude the saints of God who listened dynamically to my sermons as their pastor. Though my sermons no doubt fell short of beauty at times, our relationship as pastor and people graced by Christ redeemed them.

Dean Nadasdy

CHAPTER 1
Preaching as Art

One hears many descriptive reviews of a sermon, but they rarely include the word *beautiful*. We may describe preaching as engaging, or perhaps boring, but not beautiful. The church in its economy of words saves *beautiful* for its music and liturgy, its architecture and visual arts, not its preaching. We have separated preaching from the aesthetic.

Few preachers, after all, see themselves as artists, poets, or musicians. We may speak of the beautiful words of the Scriptures, but by the time the preacher has finished with an interpretation of these beautiful words, the product may be something less. Some of that may be due to the discipline of homiletics focusing for generations on the *how* of preaching, how to conceive, introduce, arrange, and illustrate a sermon. It has been more craft than art, at least in the mind of the seminarian and pastor. We do not usually think of our work on sermons as a work of art. Creating something beautiful hardly crosses our minds, good and true maybe, but not beautiful. Leave the beautiful to the artists, musicians, and poets.

Still, a few among us have called on preachers to see themselves, at least, as poets. Paul Scott Wilson, for example, suggests that preachers need to consider "theopoetic preaching, preaching that speaks of God in poetic ways." He writes:

> This is not preaching poems; it is poetic preaching that treasures language—with all its frail images, symbols, and metaphors—to communicate God. This sort of preaching acknowledges the fragile but powerful beauty of language, which is a critical aspect of the postmodern life.[1]

Eugene Peterson has suggested that in our talk about God, we may want to follow the conversational approach of Jesus in the Lukan travel narrative (Lk 9:51–19:27). "Tell it slant," Peterson encourages, borrowing from Emily Dickinson.[2] In other words, don't just say it, hitting listeners with truths like

1 Paul Scott Wilson, *Preaching as Poetry: Beauty, Goodness, and Truth in Every Sermon* (Nashville: Abingdon, 2014), xiv.

2 Eugene Peterson, *Tell It Slant: A Conversation on the Language of Jesus in His Stories and Prayers* (Grand Rapids: Eerdmans, 2008), 1–5.

punches, but say it poetically, using words economically, wisely, beautifully. Emily Dickinson's little verse reads:

> Tell all the truth but tell it slant —
> Success in Circuit lies
> Too bright for our infirm Delight
> The Truth's superb surprise
> As Lightning to the Children eased
> With Explanation kind
> The Truth must dazzle gradually
> Or every man be blind — [3]

Especially in sermonic communication, we preachers may still allow ourselves the easy path of theological jargon and rational argument. We distill the text into a few propositions which carry the ring of truth and make logical sense. Then we stop. We may even fatten our speech with heavy language from systematic theology. In terms of Aristotle's rhetoric, we may be strong on logos (reason) but lacking in pathos (feeling) and ethos (personal integrity). There is not much art in this approach to preaching, not much to see or feel or to consider beautiful. The beauty of an idea or a good persuasive argument may be here, but not much more.

Not to be ignored is that for centuries our preaching held a place of honor in our culture. Clergy were held in high regard. Their thoughts on matters of theology and morality were received as authoritative; the church was among our most treasured institutions. We may have bought into preaching as rhetorical persuasion, but for the most part we thought little about artistic appeal. Many preachers followed the old university scholastic model of three static points from a text and a closing poem or hymn lyric. Even then we must have seen that our sermons begged for more, and so we added that simple touch of art at the close. Most of this is gone now. Homiletics teachers saw it waning fifty years ago.

The New Homiletic, pioneered in the 1970s and 1980s by homiletical giants like Fred Craddock,[4] David Buttrick,[5] and Gene Lowry[6] proposed a corrective for the enduring practice of propositional preaching. Preachers, like it or not, were summoned to become narrative artists. Deductive preaching became inductive with elements of discovery and surprise. Sermons for centuries had focused on the preacher's theological acumen but now moved to a

3 Emily Dickinson, *The Complete Poems*, ed. Thomas H. Johnson (Boston: Little, Brown, 1955), 506.

4 Fred Craddock, *As One without Authority* (Nashville: Abingdon, 1971).

5 David Buttrick, *Homiletic: Moves and Structures* (Philadelphia: Fortress, 1987).

6 Eugene Lowry, *The Homiletical Plot: The Sermon as Narrative Art Form* (Atlanta: John Knox, 1980).

focus on the hearer's needs and experience. Those listening to the sermon were seen as its participants. Theological propositions were replaced by inductive discovery, narrative plot form, metaphor, and a variety of moves and structures. Homiletics developed a nomenclature for these changes. The propositional sermon gave way to a homiletical event or experience. The New Homiletic placed upon preachers the artistic challenges of creating a holistic, organic sermon that moved like a story. We were expected to think and speak narratively, affectively, and metaphorically. We were to "tell it slant." Sermons now went for the heart, not just the head.

Narrative preaching has been easy for some preachers and difficult for others. As one put it, "I didn't go into the ministry to tell stories, but to speak truth." Assumed here is that stark truth carries its own intrinsic value and that stories, rather than enhancing truth, distract from it. Actually, many preachers find both creating and presenting stories difficult. They may not be born storytellers nor have they received instruction in the art of storytelling. They may not think narratively. This, coupled with the valid concern for staying ever close to the scriptural text, still leaves many sermons without the beauty and engagement of story. Yet those of us who choose not to use story and metaphor in our preaching need to reread the prophets or Jesus's Sermon on the Mount. We are missing something, something engaged by the biblical text itself, and something beautiful.

In recent years, some have challenged the character, quality, and impact of narrative preaching. In 2009 Thomas Long wrote:

> What has been for the last thirty years called narrative preaching has too often developed into a hodgepodge of sentimental pseudoart, confused rhetorical strategies, and competing theological epistemologies. Preachers have larded sermons with silly stories of their pets and their children, told anecdotes from the playground to illustrate Golgotha, told hundreds of stories about certain kinds of people and shut out others, and crafted shifty trapdoor plots to keep the listeners amused. If the effect of the recent critiques is to burn away this kind of story stubble, then burn, baby, burn.[7]

Long was not suggesting that narrative preaching should be discarded for all of its sloppiness in practice. In fact he sees a "chastened, revised, theologically more astute, and biblically engaged form of narrative preaching" enduring in the future.[8] He adds this caution:

> Perhaps the most reliable measure is whether the life of the church is nourished by such preaching and finds itself more and more formed in

7 Thomas G. Long, *Preaching from Memory to Hope* (Louisville: Westminster John Knox, 2009), 25.

8 Ibid.

> the image of Christ. Faithful preaching is not story time. It is instead the spoken word at the epicenter of a community of courageous testimony. Such preaching models the vocabulary, the hospitable style of talking, the humility, the prayerful seeking, the awareness of ambiguity, the confident hope, and the gospel-storied shape of the lives of people who will talk to their children about their faith and bear witness in the world to the overwhelming generosity of God.[9]

Long's valuable insight sees meaning and beauty in the product of a sermon, the life of the transformed listener. This suggests another transition in homiletics—the move of a sermon's goal from cognitive persuasion to the transformation of the hearer. Sermons are about change, or in Long's language above, the church "finding itself more and more formed in the image of Christ." We are to imagine the world of our hearers before the text has its way with them and afterward. Our sermons are to be reflections of these two worlds, mirroring the transformation of our listeners in real time by the word we preach.[10] In every sermon, hearers are meant to experience repentance and faith within the dynamic of the law and the gospel. This is not just a cognitive exercise. It engages the emotions and the behavior of the listener, individually and in community. Each biblical text can reorder or reconfigure our listeners' experience. The preacher's role is to help listeners to see life and live life differently because of the text, and not just differently, but in a way that makes them more like Christ.

This brief review of homiletical shifts is meant to show how increasingly preachers have been expected to bring artistic elements to the homiletical task. We may not like it. We may retreat to a simple restatement of the text or to a short list of doctrinal truths. As soon as we seek to interpret a text, however, as soon as we work to interest and engage the hearer, at the point where we engage the listener's imagination to "see" a biblical text, just then our preaching has become art. So call us artists. In the telling of a story, in the unfolding of an idea, in the economic use of language, in plotting our sermonic moves, we are artists. Making and presenting a sermon is a work of art and, at its best, can be described as beautiful.

That said, we must not take ourselves too seriously. We do not necessarily need more articles on the aesthetics of theology or on the artful work of making sermons. There is always the danger of making too much of our

9 Ibid., 26.

10 Long builds on the poetics of Paul Riceour, whose thought on the interpretation of texts has significant import for preachers. See Paul Riceour, *Time and Narrative,* Vol. I (Chicago and London: University of Chicago Press, 1984); Vol II (1985); Vol III (1988). For a recent use of Riceour in the task of preaching, see Lance B. Pape, *The Scandal of Having Something to Say* (Waco: Baylor, 2013).

artfulness. Sermons can sound like essays or film reviews, like elitist art divorced from life. The best way to handle the news that preachers are artists is to go to work with the preaching task. To call a preacher an artist is simply to say that preaching is a creative task. We do not create ex nihilo, however. We imagine, shape, and give texture to what God has placed before us—a text, already, as we will see, beautiful, good, and true in itself.

American artist Barnett Newman (1905–1970) is quoted as saying, "Aesthetics is for art as ornithology is for the birds."[11] Hardly an affirmation of aesthetics! Just as an overdone emphasis on our theological purity can turn us into Pharisees, making too much of our aesthetic prowess as preachers can lead to pride, prejudice, and an elitist separation from our hearers. We can become too impressed with our creativity. The current surge of studies in aesthetic theology, however, does provide preachers with a valuable appreciation for the role of beauty in our Christian faith and witness. The caution here is that we must do the work of the preacher-artist, not just study it or discuss it. With every sermon a blank canvas awaits our artistry, usually on a weekly basis, if not more often. Truthfully, many weeks we barely have time for the work. Aesthetic theology may not be "for the birds," but it is a discipline of luxury. It is worth a look, but to do the creative work well is more important. As we do the work, let us not hesitate to call it beautiful and the work of an artist.

THE PREACHER AS ARTIST

Beginning in 1890, Claude Monet spent one year painting giant stacks of wheat just outside his home in Giverny, France. The result was the iconic series of about twenty-five paintings titled "Haystacks" (French, "Meules," stacks). He returned again and again over that year to paint the same stacks of wheat in different seasons and at different times of the day. He might set up his canvases as early as 3:30 in the morning. The tall stacks of hay on the outside kept the wheat, barley, or oats dry until the threshers came, often months later. These particular stacks belonged to Monet's neighbor but could be seen just outside his door in Giverny. The story goes that he would call for his children to bring him two or more canvases at a time as he tried to match the time and the light of each canvas with the stacks and atmosphere before him.

11 Quoted by Arthur C. Danto in *The Abuse of Beauty: Aesthetics and the Concept of Art* The Paul Carus Lectures Series 21 (Peru, IL: Open Court, 2003), 1.

Claude Monet, *Stacks of Wheat (End of Summer)*, 1890-1891,
Art Institute of Chicago, Chicago, Illinois
SEE PLATE A FOR FULL-COLOR IMAGE

Claude Monet, *Stacks of Wheat (Sunset, Snow Effect)*, 1890-1891,
Art Institute of Chicago, Chicago, Illinois
SEE PLATE B FOR FULL-COLOR IMAGE

The paintings have all survived but today are spread across the world. Eight are owned privately, and the rest are in such museums as the Metropolitan Museum of Art, the Musee d'Orsay, and the Art Institute of Chicago.[12] In 2019, one of the paintings sold at auction for $110.7 million.

12 The six paintings in the series at the Art Institute of Chicago include these: *Stack of Wheat*, 1890/91, *Stack of Wheat (Snow Effect, Overcast Day)*, 1890/91, *Stack of Wheat (Thaw, Sunset)*, 1890/91, *Stacks of Wheat (End of Day, Autumn)*, 1890/91, *Stacks of Wheat (End of Summer)*, 1890/91 and *Stacks of Wheat (Sunset, Snow Effect)*, 1890/91. For comments from Monet himself on the series of paintings see Seth Riess, "A Few Thoughts from Monet on Those Stacks of Wheat," *New Yorker* (February 25, 2015). Online: https://www.newyorker.com/humor/daily-shouts/a-few-thoughts-from-monet-on-those-stacks-of-wheat

The thought of Monet heading out once again to paint the stacks of Giverny is an apt metaphor for the preacher as artist. Like Monet, we know our subject, our text. It is familiar territory, as close as yesterday or just three years ago. We return to the same lectionary texts often. These texts are home to us. We live in them cycle by cycle. They are texts but so much more. They are the symbols that carry who we are and what we believe. Monet saw in the haystacks of Giverny an image that stood for the strength, durability, and wealth of the French farmer at a time when industry was changing everything. We come to a text expecting truth and a beauty all its own, and, like Monet, we will help people to see it.

Every time we preach from the same text, we see something new or different. Monet saw an atmosphere, a light, a texture he hadn't seen the last time. Over time, the stacks looked different, even in their color. Over time, our texts look different as well. It's the same text, that is, the word endures and does not change, but we see it differently this time around. The text stands fast, but the light and the atmosphere around it change. In preaching, as in visual art, there is always more beauty and truth to see. So we keep going back to these texts to see them again in a new way. For the longtime preacher who saves manuscripts of past sermons, it is amazing to read four or five sermons on the same text preached over twenty or more years, perhaps to two or three different congregations. How the light and atmosphere change as we work these texts "until the thresher comes!"

Like Monet, preacher-artists carry a deep desire to be faithful to the truth. For Monet it was the truth about wheat stacks. For us it is the truth of a familiar text and the changing world around it. We want our sermons to reflect the reality of our text. We strive for accuracy (getting it right) but also affect (capturing in words the beauty of the text). Like Monet looking at his stacks to see them as they truly were, we look deeply into a biblical text to see the truths of God.

SEEING THE TEXT

Preaching is as much seeing as it is talking. In Hebrew, *dabar* refers to a spoken word, but it can also be an event. The same is true for *logos* in the Greek. A word, certainly the word of God, is a sound to be heard, but it is also an event to be seen. At the beginning of Revelation, as John hears behind him "a loud voice sounding like a trumpet," he writes, "Then I turned to see the voice that was speaking to me, and on turning I saw . . ." He turned "to see the voice" (Rv 1:10, 12). When God speaks, we hear, but we also see. We look for things. We imagine. We picture. The words of the prophets engage our imaginations. In our mind's eye, when Jesus speaks, we picture what he says. That is not by accident. Jesus intended us to see what he taught.

The Bible is oral composition. The sermons within the Bible are oral compositions. That means the words are intentionally rich with images. We hear and see a text. Like many poems, the written word of God is image driven. To find the truth in a text we are often asked to see inside the text. Or, to put it another way, we are asked to see through the text to life as the text would have it, as God would have it. Either way, we are seeing the text, the way an artist sees a subject.

In this sense we are like Robert Frost in his poem, "The Pasture" inviting his listener to see what he has repeatedly seen:

I'm going out to clean the pasture spring;
I'll only stop to rake the leaves away
(And wait to watch the water clear, I may):
I sha'n't be gone long.—You come too.

I'm going out to fetch the little calf
That's standing by the mother. It's so young,
It totters when she licks it with her tongue.
I sha'n't be gone long.—You come too.[13]

Poetry is like that; so is preaching. We invite our hearers not just to listen to us, but to come with us to see what we have seen, to join us in an event of sound and sight. Oral composition is visual. Its language engages the imagination. The stories Jesus told are rich with images carried by his words: a city on a hill; a house built on rock; a shepherd shouldering a sheep; a dad welcoming home his runaway son; one man binding the wounds of another. The teaching of the apostle Paul in his letters is the same. His weighty metaphors for the atonement in Romans 3:21–26—justification, redemption, and propitiation—raise for his first hearers and readers pictures of law courts, slave markets, and temple sacrifices.

Literary composition based on reason must be read and reread. Essays, rich with formality and logic, are for intense study. Rational arguments can yield understanding and may even persuade into truth. Some may even find beauty in the arguing. Oral composition, rich with image and metaphor, on the other hand, moves along. Many poems, for instance, are meant not so much for reading as for listening and seeing. As such, the words come and go, and, in their passing, they are remembered primarily for the pictures they carry. One of the challenges faced by anyone who teaches homiletics at a seminary is that seminarians spend most of their time writing essays, designed for silent reading and strong argumentation. Then they arrive in Homiletics

13 Robert Frost, *The Poetry of Robert Frost*, ed. Edward Connery Lathem, (New York: Holt, Rinehart and Winston, 1969), 1. Interestingly, this poem is on the very first page of the complete collection of Robert Frost's poems, inviting the reader to see what he has seen.

I and are expected to write as they speak, to "tell it slant." The transition is not easy. It is like living in two worlds of communication. Some preachers never make it. Their sermons forever read like essays and may die like essays. They read their sermons word for word with the deliberate delivery of an academic fresh from the library. Usually, there can be little to see in such sermons, much to be heard, and very much to understand, but little to see.

To describe a preacher as an artist or a poet is to affirm both the visual nature of the texts from which we preach and the visual nature of preaching itself. The making and presenting of a sermon call on us to visualize truth and goodness with our listeners. The result can be an engaging beauty. In every sermon, listeners, after all, see their pastor preaching. In this sense, preaching is incarnational, summoning us to a beauty as real and as visible as flesh and blood.

CHAPTER II

The Beauty That Finds Us

In 1877 Gerard Manley Hopkins, a Jesuit priest, wrote his well-known poem, "Pied Beauty."

> Glory be to God for dappled things—
> For skies of couple-colour as a brinded cow;
> For rose-moles all in stipple upon trout that swim;
> Fresh-firecoal chestnut-falls; finches' wings;
> Landscape plotted and pieced—fold, fallow, and plough;
> And all trades, their gear and tackle and trim.
>
> All things counter, original, spare, strange;
> Whatever is fickle, freckled (who knows how?)
> With swift, slow; sweet, sour; adazzle, dim;
> He fathers-forth whose beauty is past change:
> Praise him.[14]

The poem is a celebration of contrasts. When Hopkins uses words like *pied*, *dappled*, and *brinded*, he wants us to see creation as rich with variety and contrast. He finds beauty in this speckled world, an amazing harmony of contrasts. More important, though, it all takes him to God. Hopkins finds in even the small juxtapositions of creation a testimony to the harmony of God "whose beauty is past change." This is itself a contrast worth celebrating! The result is affective—praise. The poem is framed with doxology.

In his essay, "The Origin of Our Moral Ideas" Hopkins wrote: "In art, we strive to realize not only unity, permanence of law, likeness, but also, with it, difference, variety, contrast: it is rhyme we like, not echo and not unison, but harmony."[15]

Aesthetic theology in its earliest conceptions has always taken Hopkins's route of moving from creation to Creator. In this sense, beauty is ascensional. If we see beauty in creation, it is only because the Creator is beautiful.

14 Gerard Manley Hopkins, *Poems and Prose* (London: Penguin Classics, 1985), 30.

15 Gerard Manley Hopkins, "The Origin of Our Moral Ideas" *The Collected Works of Gerard Manley Hopkins*, Vol. 4, ed. Lesley Higgins, (Oxford: Oxford University Press, 2006), 218–222.

Three times in the Old Testament (1 Chr 16:29, Ps 29:2, 96:6, NKJV) we are summoned to "worship the Lord in the beauty (Hebrew, *hadarah*) of holiness." God's holiness is God's otherness. Yet we are brought closer to this separate God by what we perceive as beautiful in God's creation. It is that way with seeing. As Hopkins put it, "What you look hard at seems to look hard at you,"[16] and then lifts you toward its Creator.

What follows is a rather condensed history of aesthetic theology. Its pace hardly does justice to the nuances of the chief contributors to aesthetic theology. It may feel much like roller skating through a museum. Still, along the way of this abridged history, we will see a deepening understanding of the role of beauty in the Christian faith and in the preaching of the church. Reviewed will be the contributions of the ancient Greek Platonists as well as the writings and sermons of Augustine, Thomas Aquinas, Martin Luther, and Jonathan Edwards.[17]

The ancient Greeks (Pythagoras, Plato, Aristotle, and Plotinus) set a standard framework for aesthetics which has endured for millennia. They saw in the beauties of the world a reflection of a real, ideal, and transcendent beauty, pure and otherly. They saw beauty, goodness, and truth as three great ideals, shaping human thought and experience. Beauty, they taught, helps hold the world together. They spoke of symmetry and proportion as beautiful. In his *Symposium* Plato has Socrates present beauty as the road to growth in both goodness and truth. Socrates says:

> The true order of going is to use the beauties of the earth as steps along which to mount upwards for the sake of that other beauty: from fair forms to fair practices, and from fair practices to fair notions until he arrives at the idea of absolute beauty.[18]

This move from smaller beauties to transcendent beauty, Plato is saying, is what takes us to goodness (fair practices) and truth (fair notions). Yet it is beauty that dominates.

Clearly, whether it was architecture, sculpture, mathematics, rhetoric, or ethics, beauty was a driving force. The ancient Greeks not only recognized

16 Gerard Manley Hopkins, *The Journals and Papers of Gerard Manley Hopkins, March, 1871*, Humphry House, ed. and completed by Graham Storey (London: Oxford University Press, 1959), 204.

17 For an abbreviated history of beauty in the church, see David Lyle Jeffrey, *In the Beauty of Holiness* (Grand Rapids: Eerdmans, 2017) and Brendan Thomas Sammon, *Called to Attraction: An Introduction to the Theology of Beauty* (Eugene OR: Cascade Books, 2017).

18 Taylor Marshall, "Seven Reasons to Love Thomas Aquinas: His Theology of Beauty" (January 28, 2018). See https://taylormarshall.com/2018/01/7-reasons-love-thomas-aquinas-theology-ancient-beauty.html

beauty, they employed it. It is difficult to over-emphasize the continuing influence of these classical thinkers in the development of aesthetic theology.

AUGUSTINE

It took Augustine (354–430) to identify the source and ideal of beauty as God. In book ten of his *Confessions*, he wrote:

> I asked the Earth, and it said, "I am not He!" I asked the sea and the deeps, and among living animals the things that creep, and they answered, "We are not your God! Seek higher than us!" . . . I asked the heavens, the sun, the moon, and the stars: "We are not the God Whom you seek," they said. To all the things that stand around the doors of my flesh I said, "Tell me of my God!" . . . With a mighty voice, they cried out, "He made us!" My question was the gaze that I turned on them; their answer was their beauty.[19]

Very much affected by the Platonists, Augustine called the transcendent beauty of the Greeks *God*. Or better and more emphatically, he called God by the name, *Beauty*. In his *Confessions*, he prays:

> Late have I loved you, O Beauty ever ancient, ever new, late have I loved you! You were within me, but I was outside, and it was there that I searched for you. In my unloveliness I plunged into the lovely things which you created. You were with me, but I was not with you. Created things kept me from you; yet if they had not been in you they would have not been at all. You called, you shouted, and you broke through my deafness. You flashed, you shone, and you dispelled my blindness. You breathed your fragrance on me; I drew in breath and now I pant for you. I have tasted you, now I hunger and thirst for more. You touched me, and I burned for your peace.[20]

Clearly, for Augustine, he did not find the beauty of God; rather that beauty found him. Augustine was taken by the idea of proportion or harmony as the true nature of beauty. This unity of parts and whole found its source and fullest expression in the unity and harmony within God. Beauty for Augustine was not "in the eye of the beholder," but an objective beauty, carrying its own power and integrity to affect us and answer our desires. So tied to God was beauty that Augustine could preach on an Easter Sunday:

> Question the beauty of the earth, question the beauty of the sea, question the beauty of the air, amply spread around everywhere, question the beauty of the sky, question the serried ranks of the stars, question the sun making

19 *The Confessions of St. Augustine*, Book X, Chapter VI (New York: Sheed & Ward, 1943).

20 Augustine, *Confessions*, X, 18.

> the day glorious with its bright beams, question the moon tempering the darkness of the following night with its shining rays, question the animals that move in the waters, that amble about on dry land, that fly in the air; their souls hidden, their bodies evident; the visible bodies needing to be controlled, the invisible souls controlling them; question all these things. They all answer you, "Here we are, look; we're beautiful." Their beauty is their confession. Who made these beautiful changeable things, if not one who is beautiful and unchangeable?[21]

For Augustine, like the pagan Platonists, beauty takes us increasingly to its highest ideal. Augustine, though, called that ideal *God*, whom he saw as ever pulling us upward. In his *Confessions* he wrote that God is "the Beauty of all things beautiful."[22] Augustine saw beauty's fullest expression in God, but, more specifically, he saw ultimate beauty in the Son of God, the incarnate Christ of God. In a sermon on Psalm 44, he sees in Christ the full expression of God's beauty:

> He (Christ) was beautiful in heaven, beautiful on earth, beautiful in the womb, beautiful in the hands of his parents, beautiful in his miracles, beautiful in his scourging, beautiful in his inviting to life, beautiful in his not caring for death, beautiful in laying down his life, beautiful in the receiving back, beautiful on the Cross, beautiful in the tomb, beautiful in heaven.[23]

Augustine tracks the beauty of Christ from heaven to earth and back to heaven. From the pre-incarnate Christ to the risen, ascended, and glorified Christ, and everything in between, Christ is beautiful.

Augustine did not just contemplate the beauty of God from a metaphysical perspective. He did not just write about beauty; he preached it. Like the poet Hopkins, he called his listeners to move from appreciating earthly beauty to knowing and loving the greater beauty of God, especially the beauty of God in Jesus Christ.

In aesthetic theology three transcendents or ideals define the essence of God and hold God's created universe together—truth, goodness, and beauty. In our preaching, truth and goodness predominate. We know truth when we see it, and we work hard in our preaching to unveil the truth of a text to the mind and heart of the hearer. We also preach to goodness, ethical living, condemning sin with the law and driving a change of will and

21 Augustine, *Sermons*, 241, Easter: ca. AD 411

22 Augustine, *Confessions*, III, 6.

23 Augustine, *Expositions on the Psalms*, 44.3.

24 Gerard Manley Hopkins, *Prose and Poems* (Penguin Books, 1953), 30.

behavior with the gospel. Often lacking, though, is an appeal to beauty, lifting us high into the very nature of the Creator—Father, Son, and Spirit.

Just as rare can be pointing to the beauty of Christ in our preaching. Earlier we considered Gerard Manley Hopkins's poem, "Pied Beauty." In another poem, a sonnet, "The Windhover," Hopkins catches the sheer beauty of a falcon in flight, a beauty which takes him in turn to celebrate the abundantly more beautiful Christ. As he turns from the falcon to Christ, to whom he dedicates the poem, he writes:

> Brute beauty and valour and act, oh, air, pride, plume, here
> Buckle! AND the fire that breaks from thee then, a billion
> Times told lovelier, more dangerous, O my chevalier![24]

Hopkins once said in a sermon: "There met in Jesus Christ all that can make man lovely and loveable." He went on to say, "I look forward with eager desire to seeing the matchless beauty of Christ's body in the heavenly light." Yet "far higher than beauty of the body," Hopkins said, "comes the beauty of his character." He ended his sermon by urging the congregation to praise the beautiful Christ over and over again in their hearts.[25]

In many ways, it is beauty that draws us to truth and goodness. That again is what it means to "tell it slant." Simply dropping truth directly on our listeners can lead them to confusion, quick denial, or even shock. Directly calling them to a particular kind of goodness may and likely should leave them feeling grossly and sinfully inadequate. Coming at truth and goodness, though, around the way of beauty, opens them to both. Beauty is a way to the heart. It was the way to Augustine's heart.

THOMAS AQUINAS

Nine centuries after Augustine, medieval Dominican theologian Thomas Aquinas (1225–1274) also took beauty seriously. Though he wrote no major treatises on aesthetics per se, he wrote often about objective beauty. Aquinas gave us the well-known dictum: "Beauty is that which being seen (perceived) pleases" (Latin, "id quod visum placet").[26] His dictum has caused no little stir over centuries of aesthetic theology. Some believe it leaves room for a subjective beauty. It depends, they say, on what Aquinas meant by "seen."

In 1878, Margaret Wolfe Hungerford wrote in *Molly Brown* that "beauty is in the eyes of the beholder."[27] With that insight, now a cliché, Hungerford

25 Quoted in Gerald O'Collins, "The Beauty of Christ," *The Way*, 44/4 (October 2005): 20.

26 Thomas Aquinas, *Summa Theologica*, Vol. 1, trans. Fathers of the English Dominican Province (New York: Benzinger Bros, 1948), 26.

27 Quoted in Paul Scott Wilson, *Preaching as Poetry*, 18.

anticipated a time when beauty would become both subjective and cultural. Now is that time. No longer seen as universal or transcendental, beauty has become a matter of personal taste. Paul Scott Wilson observes:

> A picture of a beautiful funnel cloud on the prairies may be horrifying to someone who has experienced a tornado. A tattoo may be beautiful but for some it symbolized gang violence. In Korea and Taiwan, a traditional fish lives up to its name, "stinky tofu," but those who love it find the taste beautiful.[28]

Of course, some beauty is subjective and cultural. Two people with informed tastes may not agree on the beauty of a piece of art or music. One may look at the winner of "The Ugliest Dog Contest" and see the "ugly" mutt as beautiful. If our time is one of relative truth and relative goodness, it is also a time of relative beauty. Yet in our preaching, we communicate a beauty that is undeniably objective, the beauty of God revealed in Christ, which carries its own power to win minds and hearts. It is the beauty Paul communicated: "For God, who said, 'Let light shine out of darkness,' has shone in our hearts to give the light of the knowledge of the glory of God in the face of Jesus Christ" (2 Cor 4:6).

This absolute beauty of God revealed in Jesus Christ carries its own force to convert, to stir, to humble, and to motivate. Still, I remember a woman who stayed after a wedding service to confront me with the question, "How could you bring the crucifixion of Christ into a wedding, such a violent, bloody image on such a beautiful occasion?" For her the cross was anything but beautiful, even in its ultimate expression of sacrificial love. Her objection did not change the beauty of the cross for me, the cross so rich with the truth and goodness of Christ. She did remind me, though, that for a world that does not know God, the absolute beauty of God in Christ can still be repugnant, foolish, and a stumbling block (1 Cor 1:21–25).

Leaning on and expanding the aesthetics of Platonic thinkers, Aquinas identified fixed elements of beauty, that is, qualities in an object by which we perceive it to be beautiful. These are integrity (*integritas*), proportion (*consonantia*), and clarity (*claritas*). He writes in *Summa Theologia*:

> Beauty demands the fulfillment of three conditions: the first is integrity, or perfection of the thing, for what is defective is, in consequence, ugly; the second is proper proportion, or harmony; and the third is clarity—thus things which have glowing colors are said to be beautiful.[29]

28 Ibid., 19.

29 Thomas Aquinas, *Summa Theologica*, trans. Fathers of the English Dominican Province (New York: Benzinger Bros, 1947), I, Question 39.

Beauty becomes known by its own exhibit of these elements. Integrity refers to the wholeness and perfection of the beautiful, how an object of beauty is what it is in the fullest sense. Proportion (due or proper proportion) speaks of beauty in terms of its parts contributing to one another and to a unified purpose. Clarity brings light and color into play, allowing beauty to be seen or heard for what it is. Splendor, brilliance, and the biblical *glory* come to mind here.

Gerald O'Collins summarizes these three elements of beauty with this:

> These three qualities of beauty—an exquisite flawlessness, a harmonious proportion, and a radiance—point to what we perceive in beautiful objects. They have a proper completeness; they display a perfect shape and order; and they enjoy a "luminosity" or the right balance of colour and light through which they stand out appropriately. We rejoice in the "radiant form" of some person, or delight in the "splendid" performance of a symphony or a great drama.[30]

Like Augustine, Aquinas basked in the beauty of Christ. In fact, it is in his discussion of the beauty of Christ that Aquinas identifies these qualities or properties of beauty. The original context of this list focuses on the relationship of the three persons of the Trinity in reference to the Son. Here is Thomas giving us a dogmatic argument for the beauty of Christ within the Trinity:

> The first of these (integrity or perfection) has a likeness to the property of the Son, inasmuch as He as Son has in Himself truly and perfectly the nature of the Father. To insinuate this, Augustine says in his explanation (*De Trin.* VI, 10): "Where—that is, in the Son—there is supreme and primal life," etc.
>
> The second (proportion) agrees with the Son's property, inasmuch as He is the expressed Image of the Father. Hence we see that an image is said to be beautiful, if it perfectly represents even an ugly thing. This is indicated by Augustine when he says (*De Trin.* VI, 10), "Where there exists wondrous proportion and primal equality," etc.
>
> The third agrees with the property of the Son, as the Word, which is the light and splendor of the intellect, as Damascene says (*De Fide Orth.* III, 3). Augustine alludes to the same when he says (*De Trin.* VI, 10): "As the perfect Word, not wanting in anything, and, so to speak, the art of the omnipotent God," etc.[31]

30 Gerald O'Collins, "The Beauty of Christ," *The Way*, 44/4 (October 2005): 8.

31 Thomas Aquinas, *Summa Theologica*, trans. Fathers of the English Dominican Province (New York: Benzinger Bros, 1947), I, Question 39.

The Son has integrity insofar as he "has in Himself truly and perfectly the nature of the Father." The Son has proportion "inasmuch as He is the express Image of the Father." Lastly, the third property (radiance, brightness, or clarity) is found in the Son, as the Word, "which is the light and splendor of the intellect . . . the art of the omnipotent God."

Four hundred years after Thomas, in 1677, a Silesian folk lyric appeared in the *Münster Gesangbuch* in Germany. The tune to which it would be wedded was likely originally sung by peasant workers in the fields of Silesia. We know the hymn today as "Beautiful Savior" or "Fairest Lord Jesus." It stands out as a hymn contemplating the sheer beauty of Christ. The hymn lyricist is unknown, but the lyrics and tune reveal the deep beauty of the person of Jesus Christ in the Christian mind and heart.

A close look at the lyrics reveals the aspects of beauty identified by Augustine and Aquinas. Christ is seen in relationship with the Father as the "Son of God," marking his beauty in due proportion to the Father. He is called the "King of creation," that is, the source and end of all created things as all things point to him. His purity (integrity, perfection) is celebrated as are his light and brightness (clarity, color, and light). The transforming result in those who follow Christ is love, service, and praise.

This focus on the beauty of Jesus Christ is too often lacking in our preaching. We do well with what Christ teaches (truth) and what Christ has accomplished (goodness), but we talk infrequently about who Christ is, that is, what makes Christ beautiful. A good question for all preachers to ask of the Christology in their sermons is this: "Why is Jesus Christ necessary here?"[32] The answer may indeed be in Christ's teachings or works, but the answer may also be in who Christ is, the identity and attributes of Christ which embody his beauty.

That said, we are wise to be cautious in our own ability to see the beauty of God or even the beauty of Christ. The notion that we can somehow ascend our way to discover more and more of God's beauty should give us pause. What we know about God's beauty is only ours because God in his mercy has revealed it to us in Jesus Christ and the Scriptures. This is where Martin Luther moves theological aesthetics to another level, the relational level, where God justifies ugly sinners and makes them beautiful.

MARTIN LUTHER

Like Aquinas, Luther's aesthetic theology is more implicit than explicit in his writings. It is there, though, not only in his stated love for and practice of the arts but also in his bringing the gospel to our understanding

32 Werner Elert suggested this as a pivotal question to ask in all circumstances.

of beauty. As the church celebrated the 500th anniversary of the Reformation in 2017, Mark Mattes gave us *Martin Luther's Theology of Beauty: A Reappraisal*.[33] The reappraisal comes with Mattes's understanding of how Luther moved beyond Augustine and Aquinas in his appreciation of beauty. Mattes shows how Luther saw value in the scholastic metaphysics of his forebears. He could see how, over against creation, integrity, proportion, and light are valuable standards for defining beauty. Over against God, though, beauty takes on a different and higher standard only available to those whom God has justified by grace through faith.

Mattes shows how, already in Luther's early Heidelberg Disputation and lectures on the Psalms, he rejected the human ability to know or define God's beauty apart from Christ. For Luther the beauty of God as revealed in Jesus Christ is only discernible by faith.[34] Apart from Christ, human beings are blinded to God's beauty by their sin. Mattes puts it this way: "Sinners who claim beauty for themselves are made ugly by God, and those made ugly by God can be remade as beautiful through belonging to Christ."[35]

Thesis 28 in the Heidelberg Disputation reads: "The love of God does not find, but creates that which is pleasing to it. The love of man comes into being through that which is pleasing to it."[36] In his proof of this thesis, Luther writes:

> Rather than seeking its own good, the love of God flows forth and bestows good. Therefore sinners are *attractive* because they are loved; they are not loved because they are *attractive*. For this reason the love of man avoids sinners and evil persons. Thus Christ says: "For I came not to call the righteous, but sinners" (Mt 9:13). This is the love of the cross, born of the cross, which turns in the direction where it does not find good which it may enjoy, but where it may confer good upon the bad and needy person.[37]

Luther sets the beauty of God and the beauty of the human being in the context of a relationship where God loves those who are ugly with sin and turns them into those who are beautiful with the righteousness of Christ. We are then both beautiful and ugly, *simul justus et peccator*, saint and sinner simultaneously.[38] What we know about the beauty of God we know

33 Mark Mattes, *Martin Luther's Theology of Beauty: A Reappraisal* (Grand Rapids: Baker Academic, 2017).

34 Ibid., 73–74.

35 Ibid., 79.

36 Martin Luther, *Career of the Reformer I*, eds. Harold J. Grimm, Helmut T. Lehmann, *Luther's Works*, vol. 31 (Philadelphia: Fortress Press, 1957), 57, [hereafter, LW].

37 Ibid., 31, 57. Emphasis is by the author.

only through our faith in Christ. God in Christ makes us beautiful despite our ugliness of sin. Only by the law do we see our ugliness; only by the gospel do we see God's beauty—and ours. Apart from Christ, God is hidden and ugly. In Christ, God is beautiful.

Luther brings humility to a conversation about the beauty of God and a warning concerning the self-idolatry of claiming that we can set standards for God's beauty. No one makes aesthetic theology more dependent on the objectivity of God's beauty than Luther. We know that God is beautiful only because God has graced us with faith in a beautiful Christ.

It is clear from Mattes's study of Luther as well that an ascendant knowledge of the beauty of God is a claim belonging to a theology of glory. It is rather the theology of the cross which takes us to beauty. In the ugly cross, a hidden God reveals divine beauty in Christ to an ugly sinner, who in turn is made beautiful by God's love received in faith.

Intriguing is Martin Luther's placement of beauty in God's relationship with the sinner. Beauty is the product of that relationship but, it seems, also the nature of the relationship. In other words, the relationship itself is beautiful. We know this by experience that goes beyond justification by grace through faith. To be loved by God as we are loved is beautiful. Relational beauty is something we celebrate in marriages and in friendships, but perhaps infrequently in our preaching and prayers. In the end, we say, what matters most to us is our relationships. That is true most of all in God's relationship with us. The beauty is that it is so one-sided with love.

Garrison Keillor said in an appearance, "I am a Christian because being a Christian is comedy. God does it all. All you must do to be a Christian is fall on your face and repent. God does all the rest. All the other religions are so complicated with so many rules. I am a Christian because it is easy."[39] Some may prefer to characterize our Christian life as both tragedy and comedy. Yet for Keillor, as for many, the gospel so trumps the law, that comedy prevails. If the comedic quality of our faith rests in God's doing it all and doing it well, while we fall on our faces, then we can also see the one-sided beauty of it all. Our preaching must see the beauty of it all—God transforming the ugly into the beautiful and, along the way, revealing the beauty of Christ.

JONATHAN EDWARDS

Jonathan Edwards (1703–1758) is best known for his sermon, "Sinners in the Hands of an Angry God," which characterized the Great Awakening in eighteenth-century America. For most, that is all they know of him. It turns

38 Mattes, *Martin Luther's Theology of Beauty*, 99.

39 Garrison Keillor in an appearance at Faribault, MN, August 24, 2019

out that Edwards was much more than a fiery preacher who had sinners hanging over hell by a thread. He was a prolific writer of seventy-three volumes of theology with beauty as the organizing principle—not divine sovereignty or justification by grace through faith, but the beauty of God.

> God is God, and distinguished from all other beings, and exalted above them, chiefly by his divine beauty. Not sovereignty, not wrath, not grace, not omniscience, not eternity, but beauty is what more than anything else defines God's very divinity. Edwards clearly believed in these other truths about God and saw all of them as upholding and displaying and connected to God's beauty. Yet none of them expresses who God is in the way that beauty does.[40]

Already in 1720, Edwards preached a sermon titled, "God's Excellencies." In the sermon he identifies seven divine attributes revealed in the Scriptures which testify to God's beauty.[41] These include God's eternality or self-existence, greatness, loveliness, power, wisdom, holiness, and goodness. In presenting these seven attributes Edwards builds an increasingly magnetic argument for God's beauty. Before he introduces the incarnation or the saving work of Jesus Christ, Edwards presents a completely beautiful God, worthy of knowing, worthy of worshiping.

Revealing his awareness of the Platonists, Augustine, and Aquinas, Edwards saw the beauty of God chiefly in the proportion or harmony of the persons within the Trinity. Beauty is seen best in the perfect harmony, mutual consent, and coordinated work of the Father, the Son, and the Holy Spirit. From his conversion, God's beauty drew Edwards toward God. In his preaching and writings, he integrated every aspect of Christian theology into the concept of divine or primary beauty.

One cannot read Edwards on the beauty of the Trinity without picturing Andrei Rublev's icon of the Trinity, painted in 1410. Pictured are the three "angels" in Genesis 18 who came to visit Abram at the oaks of Mamre. The three figures look alike, but each wears distinctive clothing. The Father, to the left as we look in, wears the divine color blue with a shimmering, ethereal golden robe. A "house" is behind the Father, "In My Father's House," Jesus said, "are many rooms" (Jn 14:2). The Son, at the center of the icon, is dressed with blue for his divinity and brown for his earthliness. Two fingers touch the table, marking his two natures, human and divine, as he points to the cup of his blood. Behind him is a tree, like an oak of Mamre, signaling

40 Perry Miller, John E. Smith, and Harry Stout, eds. *The Works of Jonathan Edwards* (New Haven, CT: Yale University Press, 1957–2008), 2, 298. Hereafter *WJE*.

41 Ibid., 10, 417–424. For selected quotes and an excellent commentary on the sermon, see Owen Strachan and Doug Sweeney, *Jonathan Edwards on Beauty* (Chicago: Moody Publishers, 2010), 25–38.

his cross and the tree of life. The third person of the Trinity wears the color blue as divine and also wears green for the growth the Spirit brings. Behind the Spirit is a mountain, signaling divine revelation and the lifting of us to higher things. The Spirit figure touches the table with power and blessing.

Andrei Rublev, *The Trinity*, 1425-1427, Tretyakov Gallery, Moscow, Russia
SEE PLATE C FOR FULL-COLOR IMAGE

The icon is a masterful depiction of the beauty of the Trinity resting in its due proportion, as each person of the Trinity contributes appropriately to the whole of God's beauty. Not to be missed in the icon is the open space at the table. As we look in, we realize that we are invited to the meal, into the mystery, to behold the beauty of God. There is room for us.

Edwards saw the beauty of God most clearly, though, in Jesus Christ. In a 1752 sermon he describes "the sight of the divine beauty of Christ that bows the wills and draws the hearts of men."[42] Christ "is the brightness of God's glory."[43] (Edwards used beauty and glory synonymously.) He could say of Christ: "He is more excellent than the angels of heaven. He is among them for amiable and divine beauty, as the sun is among the stars. In beholding his beauty, the angels do day and night entertain and feast their souls and in celebrating of it do they continually employ their praises."[44]

42 Quoted in Dane C. Ortlund, *Edwards on the Christian Life* (Wheaton, IL: Crossway, 2014), 27. I owe many of these insights into Edwards's theology to Dane Ortlund's text.

43 *WJE*, 25, 635.

44 Ibid.

Like Luther, Edwards saw a magnetic beauty in the Christian gospel. He said of the gospel: "Herein primarily exists the glory of the gospel, that it is a holy gospel, and so bright an emanation of the holy beauty of God and Jesus Christ; herein consists the spiritual beauty of its doctrines, that they are holy doctrines."[45] For Edwards the gospel carries its own objective appeal, a beauty that takes us to the very heart of God. Nowhere are we brought closer to God than in worship and in the preaching of the gospel. Here we are taken up into the beauty of the Trinity. So taken are we by the gospel that our countenance changes. We are beautified by the beauty of God.

Edwards believed that this beautified countenance is something Christian pastors must exhibit. In his book, *Edwards on the Christian Life*, Dane Ortlund summarizes Edwards's insight with this:

> A pastor, above all, is to provide for people a glimpse of the radiant loveliness of Christ. All their preaching, discipling, counseling, and administering are channels through which divine luminosity is beheld. The fundamental calling of leaders of God's people is not only to be under-shepherds of the chief Shepherd but also under-beautifiers of the chief Beautifier.[46]

I remember visiting a church and hearing a congregant describe his pastor with these words, "When our pastor preaches it is as if he has just come from talking with Jesus." I know of few preachers who consider themselves beautiful, but, for Edwards, preachers in touch with God's beauty, especially the beauty of Christ and his gospel, will show it.

For Edwards the beauty of God's creation is secondary, but valuable as a reflection of God's ultimate beauty. Seeing beauty in creation brings one closer to the primary beauty of God, Edwards believed. So, as one would expect, he spent time in creation. He took walks, he looked, and he saw. He appreciated what God had made. He used creation in his preaching and writing to point to the beauty of God. His "typological" approach to creation pointed to many everyday sights as finding their fulfillment in Christ. He wrote:

> That natural things were ordered for types of spiritual things seems evident by these texts: John 1:9, "This was the true Light, which lighteth every man that cometh into the world"; and John 15:1, "I am the true vine." Things are thus said to be true in Scripture, in contradistinction to what is typical. The type is only the representation or shadow of the thing, but the antitype is the very substance, and is the true thing.[47]

45 Quoted in Dane C. Ortlund, *Edwards on the Christian Life*, 28.

46 Ortlund, *Edwards on the Christian Life*, 32.

47 Quoted in Strachan and Sweeney, *Jonathan Edwards on Beauty*, 61. In this, Edwards reflects the way the church in the Middle Ages meditated upon creation in its moralized bestiaries, seeing the ways of God.

The lesser reflected the beauty of the greater. His sermons included references to everything from oceans to spiders. These portions of his preaching sound much like what we would expect from children's sermons today. Often, like Jesus, Edwards saw creation testifying to the greater divine truth, goodness, and beauty. Take this example from his *Notebook* entries:

> Roses grow upon briers, which is to signify that all temporal sweets are mixed with bitter. But what seems more especially to be meant by it, is that true happiness, the crown of glory, is to be come at in no other way than by bearing Christ's cross by a life of mortification, self-denial and labor, and bearing all things for Christ. The rose, the chief of all flowers, is the last thing that comes out. The briery prickly bush grows before, but the end and crown of all is the beautiful and fragrant rose.[48]

Reading the sermons and writings of Edwards leaves one with a desire to know God and Christ more intimately. Beauty draws us. God's beauty draws us into a deeper relationship. It is in the context of God's immeasurable beauty that we are brought to our knees in awe and wonder and readied for the repentance and faith called for in the gospel. For preachers, Edwards presents the challenge of appealing to the attributes of God, to God's overwhelming beauty, along the way of presenting law and gospel. It will not be hard to find those attributes. They are written across the texts of the Bible. What is more, though, Edwards challenges preachers to consider the question, "What about God draws my listener to the truth of this text?"

CONCLUSION

As one considers this brief historical review of aesthetic theology as it relates to preaching, several observations are noteworthy. First, the church's theology of beauty was influenced by pagan philosophers who sensed in the material beauty of their world a reflection of a higher or ideal beauty. Plato, Aristotle, Plotinus and others were lifted higher as they considered the beauties of their world. Their writings greatly influenced Christian writers and preachers who broke open pagan thought to put the label *God* to the highest ideal of beauty. Augustine even gave God the name *Beauty*. This breaking open, recasting the culture's thought, practice, or art often characterized the church's innovation. The design of the basilica, an ancient public building, for instance, became the design for the earliest public worship spaces. Cultural folk tunes over millennia have been broken open with Christian lyrics.

In our communities and even in our churches are people who may not know God but who appreciate beauty. They are twenty-first-century

48 *WJE*, 11, 58.

Platonists. They may fit into the category of "Nones," those who claim no formal religion, yet when they visit a cathedral or even our more humble sanctuaries, their hearts and their eyes are lifted. Poet E. E. Cummings, with his unique use of lowercase letters and punctuation, captured this well as he put this soliloquy into the voice of a little country church:

i am a little church(no great cathedral)
far from the splendor and squalor of hurrying
- i do not worry if briefer days grow briefest,
i am not sorry when sun and rain make april
winter by spring, i lift my diminutive spire to
merciful Him Whose only now is forever:
standing erect in the deathless truth of His presence
(welcoming humbly His light and proudly His darkness)
Such simple beauty is an avenue to our souls, a pathway for God.[49]

Second, we have seen in aesthetic theology an understanding of beauty as objective. That is, beauty, especially the beauty of God, carries its own magnetic power to attract or humble, threaten, or please. When we address the beauty of God in our preaching, we are engaging a powerful tool by which God draws people outside themselves into the numinous, where mystery and awe capture the heart. This is a form of beauty all its own. It is a beauty that humbles and even leaves faint. It is the beauty of Isaiah's vision in the temple (Is 6). This beauty has John falling "as though dead" at the feet of the risen, glorified Christ (Rv 1:17). C. S. Lewis describes "the numinous" with this: "You would feel wonder and a certain shrinking—a sense of inadequacy to cope with such a visitant and of prostration before it—an emotion which might be expressed in Shakespeare's words 'Under it my genius is rebuked.'"[50]

We may want to say that in our preaching beauty is a magnet. It is better to say that God is the magnet whose transcendent, perfect beauty appeals to those who already know God and to those who do not. The only reason people encounter the beauty of God is because God is self-revelatory. God wants to be known in our preaching.

Third, historically, aesthetic theology has applied the standards or qualities of beauty to the created world and to God. These standards—purity, proportion, and light—find their source in the beauty of the Triune God. In the circle dance (Greek, *perichoresis*) of Father, Son, and Spirit perfect integrity, harmony, and light are revealed. In this sense, what we believe

49 These are the first and last stanzas of Cummings's poem, No. 77, in *E. E. Cummings: Complete Poems, 1904–1962*, ed. George Firmage, (New York: Liveright Publishing, 1994), 749.

50 C. S. Lewis, *The Problem of Pain* (New York: Macmillan, 1962), 17.

to be true about beauty has its source in the very nature of God. Luther would warn us against thinking that a spiritually dead and ugly sinner could discover or find the beauty of God in the Trinity. There is no upward ascent of the sinner for Luther. The action is all God's, even where beauty is concerned. Again, if we see the beauty of the Trinity, it is because God has revealed that beauty to us. In fact, Luther would go so far as to say that only those ugly sinners made beautiful by God's grace can see the beauty of God behind God's own hiddenness (ugliness).

Finally, it cannot be overstated how, in aesthetic theology, God's beauty finds its ultimate expression in Jesus Christ. Jesus Christ is the premier revelation of God. As the writer to the Hebrews put it, "He is the radiance of the glory of God and the exact imprint of his nature" (Heb 1:3). God's beauty is fully revealed in Jesus Christ. Yet it is the crucified Christ, the "ugly" Christ, who saves us. Only in the gospel are sinners given the eyes to see Christ as beautiful. In this sense, the gospel can be said to be beautiful as well. To encourage beauty as a tool for preaching is to encourage Christology as the core of our preaching and the gospel turn as the critical, most beautiful moment in the sermon. To present the beauty of God in preaching is to present Jesus Christ.

CHAPTER III
What Makes a Sermon Beautiful?

Preachers do not necessarily start out to create a beautiful sermon. That may be a good thing. If we make beauty our goal in preaching we risk being impressed with our own artfulness. Worse, to the listener we may look and sound like someone trying to make beauty the goal of our preaching. The result may not be beautiful. We may try too hard and falter. We may sound like a stranger to our own people. To paraphrase C. S. Lewis, we may preach such heavenly sermons that they are no earthly good.

So let us say at the outset that our sermons are not perfect expressions of beauty just as nothing we do or say is perfect. Sinners preach sermons. Even marginal communicators preach sermons. Sinners and marginal listeners receive sermons. There is a falling short here, and so a necessary humility. Working to preach beautifully needs Walt Whitman's reminder:

> Be not discouraged, keep on, there are divine things well envelop'd,
> I swear to you there are divine things more beautiful than words
> can tell.[51]

To speak of a beautiful sermon clearly places a burden on the preacher to push language beyond where it can go, knowing all along that our preaching will never fully capture the beauty of God in Christ—"more beautiful than words can tell." Some of us will take the task so seriously we will weigh every word of it, and, in presenting our sermons, we may not look up from the words on the pages, for even a moment, to see our listeners. We are afraid that we may miss—and that they may miss—our amazingly beautiful turns of phrase. In the process, our listeners may never see the greater beauty beyond our words. There is room for caution in seeking to preach beautifully.

One of the paintings in Lucas Cranach's 1547 *Wittenberg Altarpiece* has Martin Luther preaching at the City Church in Wittenberg. We have what is most assuredly a beautiful depiction of Christian preaching at its best. At one side of the painting is Luther with one hand on the Scriptures and the

51 Walt Whitman, "Song of the Open Road," in *Walt Whitman, The Complete Works*, ed. Francis Murphy, (New York: Penguin Books, 2004), 178.

other pointing to the crucified Christ, who is at the very center of the piece. The loincloth of Christ is unfurled like a resurrection banner in victory.

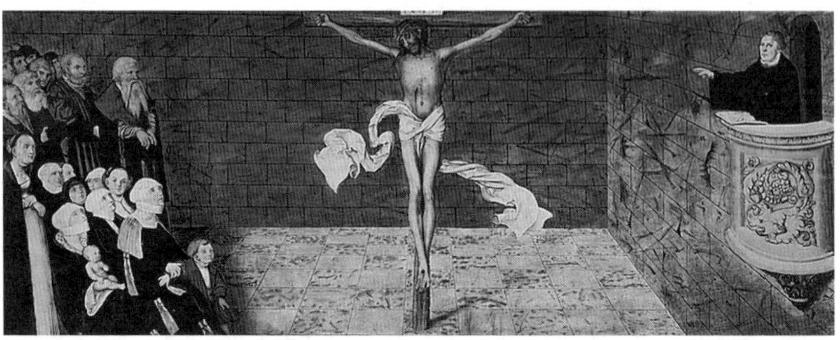

Lucas Cranach, *Luther Preaching, Altarpiece*, 1547, St. Mary's Church, Wittenberg, Germany
SEE PLATE D FOR FULL-COLOR IMAGE

At the other side of the painting are Luther's listeners, Cranach the artist among them. Members of Luther's own family are also there as listeners. If one looks closely, though, not everyone's eye is trained on Christ or the preacher. A few have turned away. They are distracted. Clearly, Cranach did not intend to make a commentary on listener distraction, but there it is, even with Martin Luther in the pulpit. So it goes with preaching. It is always less than irresistibly beautiful.

I remember as a child being captivated by a fly on the shoulder of a woman who sat in front of me in worship during the sermon. As the pastor preached I followed the fly's quick steps across the woman's back, back and forth from shoulder to shoulder. After the service, my father told me that the fly was the devil in disguise, keeping me from listening to the sermon. The thought of the devil being in church was one that had never crossed my mind. If principalities and powers are at work against the sermon, it is safe to say not all will find preaching beautiful every time.

That said, one cannot deny the aesthetic qualities of a sermon. In this chapter we will look at what makes a sermon beautiful. Specifically, we will consider seven qualities of a sermon that take our preaching toward the beautiful: God; the gospel; Christ; the word of God; worship; relationship; and an appeal to both head and heart. The preponderance of these qualities in our preaching contributes to the beauty of every sermon. As one looks at the list, some qualities clearly must be given more emphasis than others. "We preach Christ crucified" (1 Cor 1:23) places Christ and the gospel at the heart of every sermon. Still, depending on our text, one or two of these qualities may shine more than others. That variety in itself is beautiful.

After identifying and describing each of these qualities, we will also consider how a preacher might mine a specific text for the beauty it carries. Better said, we will consider how each aesthetic quality of a specific text might get the preacher's attention. Objective beauty in the Scriptures draws us in like a magnet. The story of Jesus's encounter with the disciples of Emmaus (Lk 24:13–35) will serve as our text. This lectionary text for the Easter season (the event is only recorded by Luke) gives us the intimate encounter between the risen Christ and two of his disciples, first on the road to Emmaus with Jesus as a stranger and then at home over supper with Jesus as the risen Christ.

GOD

God makes a sermon beautiful. One cannot deny the sacramental nature of preaching. Words carry the divine presence. What matters most in a biblical text is what God is doing in the text. Preachers help people remember the truths of God, and in that remembering they find hope for their future. Even more significantly, though, God actually comes to us in preaching. God speaks in the Scriptures, in the Christ, the Word made flesh, and even in the words of the preacher. People are brought into a real-time, present-tense moment of communion with God. God not only speaks in his Word; he is also present in that same Word. This presence, rich with power and purpose, is what Isaiah experienced in his call (Is 6), and it is the rain and snow of which Isaiah speaks here:

> For as the rain and the snow come down from heaven
>   and do not return there but water the earth,
> making it bring forth and sprout,
>   giving seed to the sower and bread to the eater,
> so shall my word be that goes out from my mouth;
>   it shall not return to me empty,
> but it shall accomplish that which I purpose,
>   and shall succeed in the thing for which I sent it. (Is 55:10–11)

Because God is present and purposeful in a sermon, a sermon can be said to be beautiful. The degree to which a preacher allows the text to carry the presence and purposes of God will determine the beauty of a sermon. This is not God as a concept or construct, not God as an idea or premise. This is more than the God who clinches the sermon's argument. Present in preaching is the real living God of the Scriptures. Sermons are theological. Sermons, though, are not just about God; they are God at work. Sermons are used by God to transform and sanctify God's people. What happens to a listener during a sermon is God's doing.

A sermon's beauty is derived from its carrying the presence of God. A vital task of the preacher, therefore, is to point to God as the one at work in a sermon. Sentences repeatedly have God as the subject, being and doing who God is and what God does. As the preacher points to the dynamic actions of God in the text, the attributes of God behind those actions are not ignored. Divine attributes are described, and not just described, but celebrated. A beautiful sermon brings the preacher and listeners into the beauty of God's character and activity. That beauty is not just in the past tense but in the vivid present and hopeful future perfect. It is crucial for the beauty of a sermon that it moves in real time with the character and actions of God.

In the creation of a beautiful sermon and in its delivery, God is clearly at work not only in the listeners but also in the preacher. In the preacher's own preparation, in meditation on the text, God is present. Like Jeremiah,[52] Ezekiel,[53] and John,[54] the preacher's testimony is shaped by a personal encounter with God in the text. All three of these biblical proclaimers "ate the scroll."

Preachers take texts in. In eating the scroll, the message becomes inseparable from the messenger. In a beautiful sermon there is something of the face of Moses at work.[55] The beauty of God is seen most clearly in one who has been with God. This aspect of the preacher's ethos unveils a reverent excitement over the message to be proclaimed and over the one who has placed that message in the preacher's mind and heart. To the listener the beautiful sermon comes from one who has been to the beauty of God and is still alive and eager to witness to it.

Turning to the story of the Emmaus disciples in Luke 24, the preacher here intentionally looks for the beauty of God in the text. Not to be missed is the power of God who has raised Jesus from the dead just that morning. This event comes among several post-resurrection appearances of Jesus, each one testifying to God, who raised him from the dead. God is busy here with surprise, bringing the ultimate, unexpected miracle before the eyes of these disciples. Consistent with God, whose "eye is on the sparrow," God orchestrates this divine appointment with the risen Lord for just two individuals, lesser disciples at that. And God is patient, even inductive, in revealing the risen Christ, patient through the prophets of ages past and patient with these two on their way of discovery. God shines through this text, beautiful in many ways.

52 Jeremiah 15:16

53 Ezekiel 3:1–3

54 Revelation 10:8–11

55 Moses's face shone after encountering God on Sinai (Ex 34:29–35).

THE GOSPEL

The gospel makes it possible to see the beauty of God in a sermon. In this sense the gospel becomes the primary aspect of a beautiful sermon. Affirmed here is Luther's insight that apart from the gospel sinners cannot see God's beauty. What is more, sinners have no beauty to offer God. They are ugly sinners, blind to God's beauty. God is hidden in Christ, who is anything but beautiful when one considers his cross (Is 53:3). Yet only the cross and the resurrection reveal God's true beauty to us. God makes ugly sinners beautiful by grace through faith in the gospel. The perfect righteousness (beauty) of Christ becomes ours. As Mark Mattes summarizes it, "It is the basis for their identity as Christians: God's children who are loved not because they are beautiful but instead are beautiful because they are loved."[56] Apart from the gospel, the good news of God's forgiveness in Jesus Christ, there is no seeing God's beauty in a sermon. In fact, apart from the gospel of Jesus's cross and resurrection, there is no need for a sermon. We are simply left as ugly as our unredeemed sin.

The gospel in a beautiful sermon carries overwhelming power in a dynamic tension we call law and gospel or judgment and grace. Richard Lischer has described that tension with these words:

> The preaching of the gospel—whether from the Old or New Testaments—is always dialectical. Dialectic implies two interacting forces within the unitive word of the one God, addressed to whole persons. But the dialectic is not limited to words. Israel lived out these two ways of hearing God's Word. Our preaching participates in the dialectic of salvation history, which begins with primal unity in God and moves from this original unity through one of the following sets of antitheses:
>
> chaos to order
> bondage to deliverance
> rebellion to obedience
> accusation to vindication
> despair to hope
> guilt to justification
> debt to forgiveness
> separation to reconciliation
> wrath to love
> judgment to righteousness
> defeat to victory
> death to life[57]

The Bible presents this dialectic throughout. One of the beauties of the dynamic of law and gospel is the antiphonal nature of the dialectic. The gospel is antiphonal to the law. There is the beauty of proportion here for sure, but also the beauty of a return to harmony and wholeness. The dialectic becomes a story of transformation. The bound are freed. The burdened are relieved.

56 Mattes, *Martin Luther's Theology of Beauty*, 111

57 Richard Lischer, *A Theology of Preaching: The Dynamics of the Gospel* (Durham, NC: Labyrinth Press, 1992), 33.

The broken are restored. The storylines are as many as there are listeners in a worshiping congregation. The gospel is not a cliché. It is not a one-size-fits-all panacea. Its beauty rests in its power to address real antitheses in our lives. A beautiful gospel is a personal gospel.

This calls for focused discernment on the part of the preacher. *Sin* in general hardly does the gospel justice. We look for the real struggles of our listeners, better, the ones that have a significant impact and lifespan. We don't have to look far. The text before us often reads our listeners immediately and well. The same beauty a physician finds in matching a sickness or disease with the right medicine is what we experience. It is beautiful on the giving end. It is even more beautiful on the receiving end.

One of the churches I served hosted a recovery ministry for those with ongoing addictions. It turned out that when some of these folks began attending worship, they were, from the preacher's perspective, among the most dynamic listeners in worship. They soaked up the gospel. I can't recall any of them saying, "Beautiful sermon, Pastor," but I could see it on their faces and in their worship. Recovery for them was a recurring reliance on the beauty of God's power and grace to restore and renew, and nothing assured them of those realities more than the gospel of Jesus Christ, crucified and risen. I began saying that "all of us are in recovery."

This is where hearer depiction becomes so vital for a sermon to be beautiful. Good preachers are good listeners. I asked a dinner partner once what he liked about his pastor. He paused a moment to think. I helped him along with another question. "Is your pastor a good preacher?" I asked. He smiled and said, "No, not that great, but my, can he listen! I listen to his sermons because I know he has been listening to us." The preacher's careful listening is crucial when it comes to creating a beautiful sermon. Nothing contributes more to the beauty of a sermon than the gospel of Jesus Christ appropriately applied to real questions and needs.

What saps the beauty out of the gospel? Here are some ways preachers can make the gospel less than beautiful.

Present shallow law.

Mirror specific sins which do not accuse all of your listeners. Identify "sins" which don't seem like sins or at least sins that are not that bad. Ignore the dialectical struggle, the ongoing, deep tension, which holds every listener wanting and helpless. Preaching shallow law throws a life preserver to someone standing in a puddle. The gospel is not beautiful in this case; it is perfunctory.

Present an incomplete gospel.

This is a "gospel" that fails to include one or more of the following: a Christ event or events; a clear benefit of the Christ event (freedom, forgiveness, etc.); and locality (clear instruction on where to find that benefit).[58] We have not presented a complete gospel if we state the benefit without the Christ event ("God forgives you"). We have not presented a complete gospel if we state the Christ event without the benefit ("Christ died for you"). Nor is our gospel presentation complete if we simply say, "You are baptized." That is locality, where they get the benefits, but it is not a complete gospel without Christ and those benefits.

Present a rote gospel.

To take the beauty out of the gospel, say it the same way with the same words repeatedly. "Jesus died and rose again" is one formulaic gospel. "Jesus loves you" is another. When the gospel turn arrives in a sermon, we may simply resort to our favorite formula, ignoring the dialectic which begs for a gospel directly antiphonal to the law in our sermon. If I am burdened, the gospel of the Christ event brings relief or release. If I am bound, the gospel announces freedom or recovery. If I am broken, the gospel proclaims wholeness or peace. A vivid aspect of the gospel's beauty is its symmetry with the law and its powerful narrative of change. Real people bring real needs to our sermons, in some cases needs bordering on life and death. It is no time to preach platitudes, nor is it a time for laziness. When we connect their stories of sin and finitude to a gospel tailored to their struggle, when the gospel offers real hope for their despair, genuine change for their rut, this is something beautiful.

Present the gospel with little intensity and joy.

Sometimes we present the gospel as anything but beautiful. We may peak in intensity in the application of law and present the gospel almost as an afterthought. When Paul says, "Him we proclaim" (Col 1:28), the word he uses for "proclaim" (καταγγέλλω; *katangéllo*), is more than an announcement. The "kata" prefix intensifies the word used for announce. In other words, considering the beauty of the gospel, considering the gospel's amazing power to change, we look and sound like it matters—intensely.

Fail to source the sermon's law and gospel in God.

Preaching today continues to be hearer centered. Rightfully, preachers address the hearer's needs with language and structures that work for

58 I owe this definition of a complete gospel to a treasured personal conversation with Dr. Norman Nagel, longtime professor at Concordia Seminary, St. Louis. "Christ event, benefit, and locality" are his words.

the hearer. Yet the gospel is not just something good for the hearer. It is much more than good news for a bad situation. The gospel is God's action, rich on its own with the nature and character of God. The beauty of God must shine through the gospel. Asking the question "Why?" can be helpful here. In other words, why is God so angry over sin? Why does God forgive? Why does God love me? The law does not bring judgment on sin apart from God. We don't just sin against the law. We don't just break commandments. We sin against a just, holy, and loving God. What's more, the gospel is not just an antidote for sin or a prescription for change. It is God's good news. Paul says it best when he describes the gospel as "the power of God" (Rom 1:16). Both law and gospel have their source in who God is and what God does. So every gospel presentation points to the beauty of God.

To sap a sermon of its beauty, present moralisms in place of the gospel.

Tell listeners what they *should* do or *must* do. Shame them into shape. Feed the impression of younger generations that the church is judgmental. Hold up models for good behavior and show them how short they fall from these paragons. Strike fear into their hearts. Go medieval and threaten punishment and hell itself if their lives don't come close to the Ten Commandments. Present Jesus as the ultimate good person, the model for righteous living, and let "you can be like Jesus" serve as the day's good news. If you haven't noticed by now this is law, not gospel. We can get downright ugly when it comes to trying to motivate or manipulate people.

The beauty of the gospel is that it brings its own power to motivate and to change. The gospel unfolds in the Christian life. With the preaching of the gospel comes transformation. Beautiful sermons present a beautiful gospel by telling the gospel story and by showing listeners what the gospel-driven life looks like. And it is a beautiful life.

The beauty of the gospel permeates the story of the Emmaus disciples. Most readers of Luke's Gospel already know that Christ has risen before they reach verse 13 of Luke 24. The preacher will find beauty in the transformation that the gospel brings to these two disciples—from spiritual blindness to faith, from despair to hope, from sad conversation to joyous proclamation. The gospel of the risen Christ sends them back to Jerusalem, showing beauty in its power to save and to send. The preacher will likely not address all of this beauty in a single sermon but will find a way to make the gospel turn one of the most beautiful moments of the sermon.

CHRIST

In her book *Contemplative Vision: A Guide to Christian Art and Prayer*, Juliet Benner leads her readers in quiet, prayerful contemplation of several well-known masterpieces. One of them is Caravaggio's *The Supper at Emmaus* (1601). Painted at the height of Caravaggio's career, the scene depicts the moment the disciples of Emmaus realize that the risen Lord is at their table, blessing their bread. Benner, an artist herself and a spiritual director, has us look deeply at Caravaggio's figure of Christ with these guiding words:

Michelangelo Caravaggio, *The Supper at Emmaus*, 1601,
The National Gallery, London, England
SEE PLATE E FOR FULL-COLOR IMAGE

> Look for a moment at Jesus' face. How different it is from other depictions of the Messiah before his crucifixion. And it is a different face from the one the disciples remembered. This is a young man's face—full, new, and in repose. There is individuality in this face, suggesting that this was a real model used by the artist. It is the face of an ordinary person without any signs of grandeur or heroism. Here is the face of the risen Christ, altered by the resurrection and distinguishable from the Jesus of art history. He looks not at us but at the bread before him. And

> yet we are drawn to that face. The light pulls us into the center of the painting toward the person of Jesus. How does this face of Jesus speak to you? What do you read in it—invitation, rejection, scorn, love?[59]

The light of Christ makes a piece of art beautiful. Whether it be Rembrandt's *Christ in the Storm on the Lake of Galilee* (1633) or Vermeer's *Jesus in the House of Mary and Martha* (1654, his only religious painting), the light of Christ draws us to himself.

In the 1997 film *Amistad*, two imprisoned Africans, Cinque and Minde, are given an illustrated Bible. They await trial in New England for mutiny aboard a slave ship just off the coast of Cuba. It is quiet. The light is dim. Cinque and Minde are illiterate, but the Bible gives them images through which they are introduced to Jesus. Juxtaposed in film with their discovery of Christ are the cross-centered chapel prayers of the judge in their next-day trial. Cinque and Minde respond to the images they see:

> "Their people have suffered more than ours. Their lives were full of suffering."
>
> "Then he was born and everything changed."
> (*They see the light, the corona, at Jesus's head, It is there in every picture.*)
>
> "Who is he?"
>
> "I don't know, but everywhere he goes, he is followed by the sun."
> (*They turn the pages of the Bible, looking for the next picture.*)
>
> "Here he is healing people with his hands. . . . Protecting them . . . Being given children."
>
> "What's this?"
>
> "He could also walk across the sea."
>
> "But then something happened. He was captured. Accused of some crime. Here he is with his hands tied."
>
> "He must have done something."
>
> "Why? What did he do?
>
> "Whatever it was, it was serious enough to kill him for it.
> Do you want to see how they killed him?"
> (*They see Jesus crucified between two criminals.*)
>
> "This is just a story, Yamba."

59 Juliet Benner, *Contemplative Vision: A Guide to Christian Art and Prayer* (Downers Grove, IL: InterVarsity Press, 2011), 104–105.

> "But look. That's not the end of it. (*He turns the pages of the Bible.*) His people took his body down . . . from this thing . . . this . . ." (*He draws a cross in the air. In the chapel the judge makes the sign of the cross and prays in Latin.*) They took him into a cave. They wrapped him in a cloth, like we do. They thought he was dead, but he appeared before his people again . . . and spoke to them."
>
> "Then finally he rose into the sky (*They see Jesus ascending.*) This is where the soul goes when you die. . . . This is where we're going when they kill us. . . . It doesn't look so bad."[60]

As Cinque and Minde walk to the courthouse the next day, they see the masts of ships at harbor, each one bearing the sign of the cross.

There is a compelling, objective beauty in Christ and his story in a sermon. "Wherever he goes, he is followed by the sun." Beautiful sermons are christocentric because the Bible is christocentric. In the holy history of God's people, whatever the time, the Scriptures point to Christ. Interpreting the Scriptures has always meant finding Christ in the text. The preacher is constantly asking, "Why is Jesus necessary here?" Timothy Keller puts it this way:

> The key to preaching the gospel every time is to preach Christ every time, and the key to that is to find how your particular text fits into the full canonical context and participates as a chapter in the great narrative arc of the Bible, which is how God saves us and renews the world through the salvation by free grace in his Son, Jesus Christ.[61]

Preaching Christ is more than heralding his good news. It is seeing Christ slant, telling Christ slant. It is like Caravaggio's *The Supper at Emmaus*—depicting Christ in ways that capture his beauty as a person. He is a person, after all. He is the second person of the Trinity, to be sure, but a person of astounding magnetic beauty, bearing the full image of his Father, and the most authentic person ever to walk the earth.

Some may balk at the christocentric hermeneutic, this looking for Christ in every text. If we are skeptical today of any metanarrative, who wouldn't we be skeptical of a Christ narrative? Few have met that objection more eloquently than Robert Webber who sees this hermeneutic driving the preaching of the apostles and early church fathers. Webber writes:

> The apostolic way of reading and preaching Scripture is to see Jesus Christ as the subject of the entire Bible, the subject of all history. He is

60 *Amistad*, Dreamworks Distribution LLC, 1997.

61 Timothy Keller, *Preaching: Communicating Faith in an Age of Skepticism* (New York: Penguin Random House, 2015), 70.

> the single overarching story of all time. He is the meaning of the entire narrative of human history. He is seen everywhere. . . . When I present this "Christ is everywhere in the Bible" hermeneutic to some of my pastor friends, the idea is sometimes treated with doubt, sometimes greeted with astonishment ("I've never heard that before"), but always tested with, "Where do you get that?" The answer is Jesus himself. On the road to Emmaus Jesus responds to the despair of Cleopas and his companion by pointing to the *Jesus hermeneutic* of Scripture. "How foolish you are, and slow of heart to believe all the prophets have spoken! Did not the Christ have to suffer these things and then enter his glory? And beginning with Moses and all the Prophets, he explained to them what was said *in all the Scriptures concerning himself*." (Lk 24:25–27)[62]

This Christ, the Christ of the Scriptures, is not only the subject and object of our preaching, but he comes among us in our preaching as we gather in his name. We preach a living Christ. John Frye has caught how our sermons offer hearers an encounter with Christ in real time.

> Preaching, in some traditions, is a sacrament or comparable to a sacrament. . . . Preaching is a holy event when the preacher and the preached encounter the living God together. The aim of preaching is community—encounter with the living, eyes-blazing Christ who walks in the community's ordinary, particular midst. Revelation chapters 2 and 3 are not just about the living Christ showing up a long time ago to seven churches in Asia Minor. The glorified Jesus, as Lord of his church, still walks around in the midst of local gatherings.[63]

We do not just simply preach Christ as a historic figure, but Christ present in this moment, in these words, in this place. A few years ago New York Avenue Presbyterian Church in Washington, DC, celebrated the ministry of one of its former pastors, Peter Marshall. Marshall came to the church in 1937. Ten years later he was elected chaplain of the United States Senate. He would die in 1949. The bulletin announcing the commemoration carried these words: "Peter's goal in preaching and ministry was always to make Jesus real to people, and he seems to have succeeded wildly, for as one woman enthused, 'We seemed actually to feel Christ beside us, to hear the rustling of his robes.'" Marshall would actually use the words, "the rustle of his robe" when preaching the presence of Christ. Such is the living beauty Christ brings in preaching.

62 Robert E. Webber, *Ancient-Future Worship: Proclaiming and Enacting God's Narrative* (Grand Rapids: Baker Books, 2008), 119–120.

63 John Frye, "Preaching as Encounter," http://www.patheos.com/blogs/jesuscreed/2013/05/17/from-the-shepherds-nook-preaching-as-encounter/.

John Newton once wrote a letter of encouragement to a friend. In that letter he wrote of Jesus:

> To view him by faith, as living, dying, reigning, interceding and governing for us, will furnish us with such views, prospects, motives, and encouragements, as will enable us to endure any cross, to overcome all opposition, to withstand temptation, and to run in the way of his commandments with an enlarged heart.[64]

Notice how Newton focused on viewing Christ ("To view him by faith . . ."). In many ways that is what preachers do. We help people imagine the Christ, to see him with the eyes of faith. The result is Newton's assurance of "an enlarged heart." Again, it is not talking about Christ being present; it is "seeing" his presence in real time, in the moment of a sermon. This is not the real presence of Christ in, with, and under the bread and wine of the Eucharist, but it is a promised presence fulfilled as we gather in his name (Mt 18:20).

Some offer a caution here. There can be a risk in a constant focus on Jesus Christ in our theology and preaching. Consider the reflections of Fred Craddock:

> Some in the Christian community seem content to supplant theology with Christology, but perhaps unaware of the immense price: the dislodging of Christ from salvation history, the loss of continuity with Israel's faith, the separation of creation from redemption (opening the door to every otherworldly heresy hovering around the church), and the reduction of the first item of the Christian creed to the role of preface.[65]

In other words, in focusing on Christ, it is said, we may subtly deny the role—and the beauty—of the Father and the Spirit in our faith and life. We may ignore creation themes. We may step away from our Old Testament roots. We may ignore the God of our salvation history. We may never address our Spirit-driven growth in sanctification. "Jesus only," after all, is heresy, strange as it is, claiming that Jesus is all three persons of the Trinity wrapped into one. Repeatedly preaching Christ-centered sermons can lead to a silent neglect of the complete beauty of God—Father, Son, and Spirit. Still, we take the caution and preach Christ, recognizing his place in the beautiful unity and proportion of the Trinity. As the apostle Paul told his elders in summarizing his preaching after three years in Ephesus, "I did not shrink from declaring to you the whole counsel of God" (Eph 20:27). That "whole

64 Quoted in Tony Reinke, *Newton on the Christian Life: To Live Is Christ* (Wheaton, IL: Crossway, 2015), 270.

65 Fred Craddock, "The Gospel of God," in *Preaching as a Theological Task*, ed. Thomas G. Long and Edward Farley, (Louisville: Westminster John Knox, 1996), 75.

counsel" constitutes our preaching as well, with the beauty of Christ at its core. We will be christocentric in our preaching but also trinitarian.

If one can in any way measure the times, it does seem that it is the right time to focus on the person of Christ in our preaching. I realize that it has always been the church's task to "preach Christ crucified" (1 Cor 1:23). Right now, however, nearly a quarter of the way into this century, the beauty of the person of Jesus Christ may win the heart more readily than propositions or traditions or even confessions. To say it better, the person of Jesus Christ may be the most effective way to shed light on these very treasures. If those outside the church are to find a reason to look in on us and what we believe, teach, and confess, it may be because the preaching of Christ gives them a magnetic beauty to behold, a beauty that is integrity, proportion, and light. The apostle John, who knew Jesus and loved him, could write: "In him was life, and the life was the light of men. The light shines in the darkness, and the darkness has not overcome it" (Jn 1:4-5). That is the beauty of Jesus Christ.

Just as christocentric preaching brings beauty to a sermon, it also brings goodness and truth. Christ embodies goodness and truth. He is the *good* shepherd (Jn 10:11). Paul describes Christ as "the *goodness* and loving kindness of God our Savior" (Ti 3:4). John's prologue to his Gospel describes Jesus as coming "full of grace and *truth*" (Jn 1:14). Jesus captures his own nature and function as *the truth* (Jn 14:6). To preach Christ is to present Christ as good and true. There is no need for defending here or for making a logical argument. We preach it as it is true, not as *if* it is true, but as it *is* true.[66]

In preparing a sermon on Christ's encounter with the Emmaus disciples, the preacher cannot miss the christological beauty of the text. Christ draws near and walks with them before they recognize him. As he opens the Scriptures to them on the way, their hearts "burn" within them (Lk 24:32), Luke comments that in opening the Scriptures, Christ interpreted "the things concerning himself" (Lk 24:27). This is Christ finding himself at the center of Old Testament prophecies—the beauty of the Word within the word. The beauty of Christ shows too, as, still the stranger, he accepts the disciples' invitation to supper, as if answering the prayer, "Come, Lord Jesus, be our guest." As the risen Lord blesses and breaks bread in their home, the recognition comes. They see the Lord for who he is, in all of his goodness, truth, and beauty. Christ disappears, but from his presence two new witnesses rise and go to testify that "the Lord has risen, indeed" (Lk 24:34). The beauty of the risen Christ permeates this text, not the least of which is the surprise he provides as he humbly comes at them "slant," allowing them to discover his identity. This is Christus Victor, but also Christ the companion, Christ the teacher, Christ the guest, who makes our home his home.

66 I owe this distinction to Robert Webber. See *Ancient-Future Worship*, 124.

THE WORD OF GOD

We preach from the word of God as revealed in the Scriptures. Our biblical text gives our sermon authority. Textual preaching requires that we stay close to our text. Too often for some preachers, the text appears in the first minute of the sermon and then disappears completely. In evaluating sermon manuscripts in homiletics classes, it is not uncommon to write on page two of a sermon, "Where did your text go?" We need to keep our text engaged throughout a sermon not just to maintain our derived authority but for the sake of preaching a beautiful sermon.

Isaiah the prophet writes: "The grass withers, the flower fades, but the word of our God will stand forever" (Is 40:8). A biblical text gives eternal weight to a sermon otherwise destined to be forgotten by Sunday brunch. The texts we receive for preaching come to us after centuries of use. Their dogged preservation and longevity of use by God's people speak to their beauty. We who preach and listen to sermons vouch together for these words—they are God's words. That makes them beautiful as does the genius of the stories they weave, the histories, the parables and metaphors, the songs, the gospels, the letters, and the visions. Whatever the form God has used to speak to us in the word, it moves us to imagine, pray, wonder, and love. This is why the word itself has people saying things like: "In the way of your testimonies I delight as much as in all riches. I will meditate on your precepts and fix my eyes on your ways. I will delight in your statutes; I will not forget your word" (Ps 119:14–16).

This explains why the public reading of the Scriptures continues to be a cherished moment in Christian worship. From synagogue days, the scrolls have been opened, and the God-breathed words have been read aloud. Even in synagogue worship and in the first house churches, as in liturgical churches today, texts were appointed to be read on certain days and holidays. Early on after Christ, within a century, letters and gospels were added to the readings. Then, after the readings, someone spoke from those words on their meaning and impact. Justin Martyr famously describes Christian worship in AD 150 with this:

> And on the day called Sunday, all who live in cities or in the country gather together to one place, and the memoirs of the apostles or the writings of the prophets are read, as long as time permits; then, when the reader has ceased, the president verbally instructs and exhorts to the imitation of these good (beautiful) things.[67]

67 Justin Martyr, "Apology 1," *The Writings of Justin Martyr*, ed. Philip Schaf. Text taken from Ante-Nicene Fathers, Volume I (Buffalo, NY: Christian Literature Publishing, 1885), 67. Source of the electronic version: www.ccel.org.

The beauty of the word of God—its unity and variety, its simplicity and depth—has characterized Christian preaching from the beginning. Before the preacher speaks, there is already an enduring beauty in the text.

Clearly, a sermon on Christ and the Emmaus disciples might easily find beauty in the unity of the Scriptures in testifying to Christ. On one of our tours of Israel, our local guide, a Palestinian Christian, was astoundingly well-versed in the Scriptures. His lectures at various Holy Land sites were peppered with Old Testament prophecies fulfilled in the life of Christ in the New Testament. I watched and listened as Christian pilgrims were wowed repeatedly by these connections, showing the christological consistency of the Bible over centuries of history. I don't know if I have ever been more stirred by the beauty of the Scriptures than in those lectures. Such a stirring happens in this text, both for those inside the text's story and those whom the text engages. Of course, the preacher who celebrates this particular beauty in the text will be careful not simply to point it out but to show hearers what it actually looks like—the Bible in its beautiful unity of promise and fulfillment.

WORSHIP

We do not preach in a vacuum. The sermon is embedded in the beauty of worship. Preaching is worship itself as God moves in the word with grace and truth. Sacred space sets preaching into a beauty that seeks to reflect the holiness of God. As Psalm 96:6 sings it: "Splendor and majesty are before him; strength and beauty are in his sanctuary." The worship space may provide a metaphor for our identity as we gather in cruciform or in a circle broken open by a table. Many worship settings lift the eyes of worshipers to a cross or to an image of Christ. The table, the font, and the Book visualize God's actions among us. Beautiful sermons now and again point to these visual references, marking the locality of God's grace among those who worship.

Churches may have stained glass or other works of visual arts which periodically make their way into sermons. To enhance a sermonic move, a work of art may be referenced and described. One of my earliest memories from childhood recalls my pastor describing the stained- glass window right next to where I sat. I hung on every word he spoke as he gave meaning to the trinitarian symbols at work in the window's images. If the church has a screen, an imported art piece may be displayed. Otherwise the preacher describes the piece verbally, knowing that later that day many will search for the piece on the Web. In the next chapter, we will address the use of visual art in preaching.

The historic liturgy's Ordo provides a beautiful pattern for our worship. Gordon Lathrop has highlighted the genius of the juxtapositions of worship acts arranged to complement one another.[68] There is sense to this order, and not just sense, but a beauty of apposition, proportion, wholeness, and harmony that builds to one summit and then to another. Along the way of the liturgy God encounters us not once but several times in the law and the gospel. In historic worship we experience baptism with teaching; confession and absolution with praise; the readings broken open with meaning by the sermon; the sermon unfolding in a response of the creeds and the prayers of the church. We prepare for the meal with our offerings and thanksgiving. Christ comes to us in his meal. We depart with prayer and blessing. At any time in the sermon, the pastor may pick up the familiar words of a "Kyrie" or a "Sanctus" or simply a "Thanks be to God," offered now in a fresh way. In doing so, there is added beauty to the preaching.

The liturgy's propers mark the unique times and seasons of the church. We move in preaching with the church's cadence and calendar. We receive biblical texts of the seasons. We speak with seasonal language, using words like waiting, incarnation, glory, repentance, life, and growth to mark the time. Any day of worship is seen in relation to all other days leading to and flowing from the Feast of the Resurrection, the center of our year together. This cadence, this different time, pervades our preaching. We gather at the turn of the week, setting our worship in apposition to the seven days to follow until we meet again. Monday and the mundane are on the mind of the preacher whose words are timed and tuned to the daily life which follows the Eighth Day of worship. It is all very beautiful.

The beauty of music also surrounds our preaching. We sing our prayers, praises, and even our dogma. The apostle Paul summons Christians to "let the word of Christ dwell in you richly, teaching and admonishing one another in all wisdom, singing psalms and hymns and spiritual songs, with thankfulness in your hearts to God" (Col 3:16). Our music may be as diverse as "psalms, hymns, and spiritual songs." Choirs, ensembles, and solos ready people for the word and help to shape their response to it. So close, so complementary, are the sermon and the music in worship that the preacher may call the listeners to join in song even during the sermon. Some lyrics of the church's song are so cherished that they are known from memory, even by those on the edges of the church's fellowship. "Amazing Grace" is one of those. "Blessed Assurance" and "How Great Thou Art" are two other examples. Anyone who remembers singing hymns at a Garrison Keillor *Prairie Home Companion* radio program knows the power of hymns to be

68 Gordon Lathrop, *Holy Things: A Liturgical Theology* (Minneapolis: Augsburg Fortress, 1993), 15ff.

recalled and treasured. In my experience, congregations develop a list of favorite hymns and songs, which may be over-sung by some estimates but still seem to carry an incredible sense of beauty and of being at home in worship.

The story of Jesus and the Emmaus disciples suggests the beauty of worship in the presence of Christ. Here Jesus fulfills his own promise, "For where two or three are gathered in my name, there am I among them" (Mt 18:20). The risen Christ comes to us, and his coming turns supper for two into beautiful worship. With his presence comes the truth of the resurrection every time we worship, at home or in our church's sanctuary. Preaching here with a heart for the beauty of worship may lead the preacher to invite the singing of an appropriate hymn ("Abide with Me," for example) during the sermon or to develop a call and response throughout the sermon, such as "Come, Lord Jesus, be our guest."

RELATIONSHIP

Surrounding every preacher is an array of contexts, each of which brings its own beauty to a sermon. A congregation's unique culture, its liturgy, and its confession all contribute to make a sermon beautiful. The pastor's own personal life can lend beauty to a sermon as can the history of his predecessors in the congregation's pastoral office. Of all the preaching contexts, though, the relationship of preacher and listener contributes most to making a sermon beautiful. The longer one serves in ministry the more one senses the beauty of the relationship between pastor and people. What often lingers in a retired pastor's memory, for instance, are not the endless meetings or even the difficult conflicts along the way. What lasts in memory are the cherished relationships of pastor and people, remembrances that span space and time.

The preacher addresses listeners as their pastor. The sermon is preached in a relationship where mutual trust has been earned over time. The pastor is not just the listeners' preacher but their shepherd. Preaching may be the most public of a pastor's acts of service, but it may not be the most treasured. As the pastor preaches, the voice heard is the same voice which has spoken prayers and encouragement in the pastor's office, the listener's home, or in hospital. It is also the same public voice of the Bible study teacher, the voice at the communion rail and the font, the voice prompting the wedding vows and bringing peace at the time of death. As it was with Jesus, it is with pastors; a pastor's flock knows the pastor's voice, "he goes before them, and the sheep follow him, for they know his voice" (Jn 10:4).

The literature in homiletics has to a large extent ignored the impact of pastoral relationships on the preaching task. These relationships are what make the sermon encounter much more than just speaking and listening. The preacher and listener have a history outside of the sermon. At its best, it is a beautiful history of care, trust, in some cases, endurance, and, above all, a shared, personal experience of the presence of Christ. For most preachers, the right to be heard has been forged in the trenches of pastoral ministry.

In Marilynne Robinson's Pulitzer-Prize winning *Gilead*,[69] John Ames is a small-town pastor in Iowa, writing a memoir for his son. Along the way, Pastor Ames has navigated his personal struggles, loneliness among them and deep loss as well. Yet beaming from his memoir is a touching humility and an appreciation for the people he has served in pastoral ministry. There is, in the end, serenity for Pastor Ames, who never takes himself seriously enough to do damage to souls or to himself. He describes one of his dreams: "I was preaching to Jesus himself, saying any foolish thing I could think of, and He was sitting there in His white, white, robe looking patient and sad and amazed."[70]

I remember stopping at this passage in *Gilead* and recalling how my pastoral relationships could all be placed in the circle of relationships we mutually had in Christ. Unlike Ames, there were no fertile dreams. Sometimes, though, I was acutely and wondrously aware of his presence in moments of pastoral care. At other times, it was in preaching that I "saw" him. The point is, he was there whether I recognized him or not. At the center of my circle of friends in ministry, whether wide or small, was Christ.

In *Reading for Preaching*, Cornelius Plantinga, Jr. briefly discusses the character of Pastor Ames and provides this beautiful affirmation: "Ames celebrates the sacrament of sheer existence in his church members, treating each as unrepeatable. Each, to him, is an unrepeatable and incandescent divine thought."[71] This kind of respect and love toward one's listeners goes a long way in establishing the ethos of a pastor and preacher. It is the splendid work of the Holy Spirit gathering the church around the Christ, and it is beautiful.

One cannot read *Gilead* without thinking of George Bernanos's *Diary of a Country Priest*.[72] Here an unnamed young priest in pre-World War II rural France struggles with an antagonistic culture, town gossip, chronic

69 Marilynne Robinson, *Gilead* (New York: Farrar, Straus, and Giroux, 2004). For an appreciation of this character in Robinson's book, see Cornelius Plantinga, Jr., *Reading for Preaching* (Grand Rapids: Eerdmans, 2013), 84–85.

70 Robinson, *Gilead*, 68.

71 Plantinga, *Reading for Preaching*, 85.

72 George Bernanos, *Diary of a Country Priest* (New York: Macmillan, 1937, 1965).

illness, personal faith questions, and what seems to him to be a life without impact. Along the way, he was struggling with cancer. Yet what we see in his relationships with his parishioners is a relentless desire to be their pastor. In a pivotal pastoral visit with the wealthy Countess Mme la Comtesse, the young priest listens as she pours out her anger over losing an eighteen-month-old son. Together they weep. Miraculously, along the way of their encounter, he finds these words to say: "But you know that our God came to be among us. Shake your fist at Him, spit in His face, scourge Him, and finally crucify Him: what does it matter? It's already been done to Him."[73] Near the end of their visit, Mme la Comtesse kneels down and releases the hurt and anger she has carried, and her pastor blesses her. Later she observes in a letter to him: "I have lived in the most horrible solitude, alone with the desperate memory of a child. And it seems to me that another child has brought me to life again."[74] The beauty of these pastoral moments, accompanied by every pastor's experience of boredom, loneliness, turmoil, and conflict, leave pastor and people with a deep appreciation of their life together. It is said best by the words of Bernanos's young priest on his deathbed: "Grace is everywhere."[75]

The beauty of the pastor/people relationship is more than aesthetic. It explains how the preacher's sermons reveal such an intimate awareness of the listeners' lives. People may leave church and say at the door: "Have you been reading my email messages lately?" or "How did you know I needed exactly that sermon this morning?" This reveals a beautiful harmony between word and life. The shepherd knows his sheep, Listeners hear their preacher sounding like their pastor—speaking with the same gentle love and concern for their cherished souls. It has become a cliché, but the old advice given to preachers still holds—"they will not care how much you know until they know how much you care."

Well-known preacher Andy Stanley has suggested a structure for preaching that builds on the relationship of pastor and people.[76] His relational pattern sets the focus of a text in the relationships among preacher, listener, and God. The first move (ME) has the preacher introducing a topic from the text and why, for the preacher, it is personally engaging or disturbing. The second move (WE) shows how the community of listeners relates to the topic, its significance for them. The third move (God) sheds light on what God has to say on the issue or topic from the biblical text. In the fourth move (YOU) the preacher speaks to each

73 Ibid., 185.

74 Ibid., 188.

75 Ibid., 317.

76 Andy Stanley, *Preaching for a Change* (Colorado Springs: Multnomah Books, 2006).

individual listener, applying God's word to the individual's experience. Finally, it's back to the community of listeners (WE), motivating them to respond to the truth of the text. Stanley shows how a preacher can take one of the significant beauties of preaching—relationships—and use it as a pattern for structuring a sermon.

There is one more aesthetic aspect to the relational side of preaching. Drawing from traditional African American preaching, Evans Crawford has presented the relationship between preacher and listeners as strongly dependent on the preacher's "homiletical musicality." This is more than a sermon being beautifully accompanied by music. It is the actual music of preaching. Crawford celebrates the orality of preaching, especially its musical qualities, in the traditional Black church. Crawford refers to "the way in which the preacher uses timing, pauses, inflection, pace, and the other musical qualities of speech to engage all that the listener is in the act of proclamation."[77] A congregation moves with its preacher through a series of oral responses, from "Help them, Lord" to "Well?" to "That's all right!" to "Amen!" and, finally to "Glory Hallelujah!" These "starters and sustainers" are prayerful, seeking, and celebrative responses, moving the preacher and listeners along through the sermon together. There may be a pause for prayer, or a mood change in anticipation of the next move. The preacher may provide a repeated riff which listeners pick up and chant. The beauty is in the harmony and the symbiosis of speaker and listener, listener and speaker. This is "the Hum" of call and response preaching. It is preacher and people firing on all cylinders. It is "an expression of the holy God working through the preacher and community, and it requires a rigorous and authentic spirituality on the part of both preacher and congregation."[78]

Certainly the artful beauty of "the Hum" has its source in the oral tradition of enslaved African Americans, who found each other in worship together. We must see it, though, as more than the vestiges of folk art. What happened for generations in this preaching culture was an experience of the church at its most effective and inspirational moments. Preachers do not need to be afraid of call and response. It can be a simple textual refrain or a "Lord, have mercy!" We can learn from this artistic tradition. We can learn to watch and listen to our congregation of listeners. We can ask them questions. We may not get audible feedback from them, but we

77 Evans E. Crawford with Thomas R. Troeger, *The Hum: Call and Response in African American Preaching* (Nashville: Abingdon, 1995), 16. Crawford credits Jon Michael Spenser with coining the term, "homiletical musicality" in Jon Michael Spenser, *Sacred Symphony: The Chanted Sermon of the Black Preacher* (Westport, CN: Greenwood, 1987) and *Protest and Praise: Sacred Music of Black Religion* (Minneapolis: Fortress Press, 1990).

78 Ibid.

can watch for "feelback" on their faces and in their body language. We can pause and look at them. We can pause and pray with them. "The Hum" points to the beauty of the relational partnership which must exist for preaching to have its way in the church and community. It reminds us that preaching is communal, beautifully communal. Sermons may not span space and time like the Eucharist, bringing preacher and listeners into the realm of angels and archangels, but within space and time, the sermonic hum reveals a congregation's deep relational harmony in Jesus Christ.

The beauty of relationship certainly shines through Luke's account of the Emmaus disciples. Jesus enters their conversation. His patience and deference toward the disciples are amazing. He lets them tell their story. At first the disciples appear as the ones in the know with the stranger needing an update on the latest news from Jerusalem regarding Jesus of Nazareth. Their update includes much accurate detail in reporting the events surrounding their teacher's death and the disappearance of his body. They state their deep disappointment. "We had hoped that he was the one" (Lk 24:21), they say. Jesus responds with a gentle rebuke, but that rebuke is eclipsed by his turning the conversation into a teaching moment from the Scriptures. Jesus does not simply reveal himself to the disciples and say, "Don't you recognize me? Here I am! It's Jesus!" Rather, he reveals himself in the Scriptures and in the breaking of bread. In the process, he establishes a relationship with these disciples rich with grace and revelation. He is not just "the one to redeem Israel" (Lk 24:21); he is their risen Lord.

Texts like Luke 24:13–35 are crucial texts for the church's preaching witness today. Many today will come to faith not so much through doctrinal argument or apologetics but through the presentation of a relational Christ. Like the Emmaus disciples, many need to know, in a very personal way, the Christ of walks and transitions, the Christ of conversations, the Christ who enters our disappointments and makes himself at home with us. This beautiful Christ of relationships will be for many the way into the kingdom. People today still ask the question, "How can you be sure that Christ has risen from the dead?" A first inclination is to argue from the proofs of the resurrection, many of them quite convincing. Another line of response, though, simply says, "I know he is alive after dying because I just spoke with him."

HEAD AND HEART

The beauty of a sermon is a matter of both head and heart. The preacher as artist appeals to the intellect and the emotions of the listener. Even today in a screen culture, listeners know a good oral argument when they hear one. They find beauty in thinking through the sermonic moves with their preacher. How each part moves the sermon along in a logical and persuasive way, contributing to an organic whole, engages the hearer's cognitive tools. In other words, a sermon's beauty is enhanced when it makes sense. No doubt this is behind the apostle Paul's prayer request as he asks the Colossian Christians to "pray also for us, that God may open to us a door for the word, to declare the mystery of Christ, on account of which I am in prison—*that I may make it clear,* which is how I ought to speak" (Col 4:4–5). Clarity of speech and of argument matters. Preachers who value beauty must not assume the clarity of their speech. We are often discussing matters alien to everyday conversation and using a vocabulary unfamiliar to many. Beautiful sermons present convincing arguments, skillfully woven. Preachers work at precision. Many are skilled wordsmiths.

A caution here: It is amazing how we preachers can cast a dark shadow of confusion over a radiantly clear biblical text. Texts carry their own clarity. The perspicuity of the biblical text is one of its treasured qualities. Yet, as we quickly run to a topic from a text or as we ask several questions of a text, the sharpness of the text may become blurred, its clarity dulled. Preaching textually means preserving the profound, but also, the often-simple meanings a text carries. Maintaining this kind of clarity is not lost on listeners, but it is hardly enough.

A beautiful sermon also appeals to the listener's heart. It takes a truth or concept and makes it real for the listener. Jonathan Edwards said it this way:

> There is a difference between having an opinion that God is holy and gracious, and having a sense of the loveliness and beauty of that holiness and grace. There is a difference between having a rational judgment that honey is sweet and having a sense of its sweetness. A man may have the former that knows not how the honey tastes, but a man cannot have the latter unless he has an idea of the taste of honey in his mind.[79]

In his book *Preaching*, Tim Keller highlights the contribution of Jonathan Edwards to religious psychology, especially where head and heart are concerned.[80] In *The Religious Affections*, Edwards identifies two faculties of the human soul: understanding and inclination. Understanding involves a perception and a cognitive grasp of the nature of things. Inclination is our will and heart at work to accept or reject what we perceive. Affections, Edwards says, are a crucial aspect of inclination. Our affections,

79 Quoted in Timothy Keller, *Preaching: Communicating Faith in an Age of Skepticism* (New York: Viking, 2015), 162–163. Jonathan Edwards, "A Divine and Spiritual Light," in *Jonathan Edwards Reader* (New Haven, CT: Yale University Press, 1995), 112.

80 Ibid., 160–161.

often rich with emotions, involve convictions of the mind and real changes in life. For Edwards, understanding and affection were not contradictory, but complementary.

So one of the beauties of preaching is how it engages both head and heart. We preach cognitive truth and understanding but we also preach to the heart, experience, and attitudes of our listeners. We strive not just for belief but for life based on the belief. This was the intention of the New Homiletic, which is not very new anymore. The cognitive propositions shaping sermons were too often distinct from the heart language of metaphor, story, analogy, and image. We strove for understanding and often failed at inspiration and affection. Fifty years later, we can see how preaching must not go exclusively for the heart, how the on-going transformation or sanctification of the Christian involves both head and heart. When we interpret the truths of a text with the language of narrative and image or with an attitude of wonder and mystery, we deepen the beauty of our preaching.

Where beauty is concerned, how we tell the story of a text matters. The story of the risen Lord's encounter with the Emmaus disciples begs for both head and heart to be engaged. That is what happens in the text itself. Jesus argues from the Scriptures to show how the prophecies are fulfilled in him. Along the way of conversation, the disciples' hearts burn with wonder and emotion. The story includes teaching and blessing, proof and wonder, recognition and surprise, explanation and exuberant proclamation. The text's mix of head and heart language presents a beautiful story that lingers in memory. A beautiful sermon will do no less.

CHAPTER IV
The Use of Image in Preaching

Rembrandt van Rijn, *Christ Preaching (La Petite Tombe)*, ca. 1652, Rijksmuseum, Amsterdam, The Netherlands
FEATURED ON THE FRONT & BACK COVER

EKPHRASIS

In Rembrandt's etching, *Christ Preaching*,[81] Christ proclaims the kingdom in an intimate setting surrounded by enrapt listeners. It is clearly a moment of engagement. As one looks more closely, though, a smile comes easily. Rembrandt has placed at the center of the foreground a little boy who draws with his finger in the dirt. A ball of string, his toy, is at his side. An earlier, better-known engraving, *The Hundred Gilder Print*,[82] also shows Christ preaching but without the little artist in the foreground. So what to make of the child doodling while Christ preaches? Why has Rembrandt added this figure to the scene? Some see it as comic relief, a humanizing of

81 Rembrandt van Rijn, *Christ Preaching* (ca. 1652), etching, drypoint, and engraving on laid paper, 28.1 x 39.8 cm, Rijksmuseum, Amsterdam.

82 Rembrandt van Rijn, *Christ Preaching (The Hundred Guilder Print)* (ca. 1646–1650), etching and drypoint, 28.1 x 39.8 cm, Rijksmuseum, Amsterdam.

an extraordinary event. No doubt, it has this effect. If we could make out the boy's drawing in the dirt, perhaps we would see a primitive portrait of Jesus or, who knows, something totally unrelated to the sermon. Since I first saw the piece, though, I have always seen the child as an affirmation of Christ's artistic prowess as a preacher. I may be optimistic here, but I would like to believe that Christ has couched his gospel in language so visual that we might see in the dirt a primitive drawing of a wooly sheep escaping the fold or a treasure in a field. If this were so, maybe Rembrandt is showing us how Jesus's preaching was image-driven, how artists, even the youngest among them, find something to see in Jesus's sermons. Rembrandt certainly did. His depictions of biblical scenes are rich with meaning. Just as likely is that Rembrandt has given us an image of himself as a child artist depicting what he hears and sees on a dirt canvas.

That is one way it goes—from words to image. Visualization has preserved the spoken word for generations. Words give birth to image. With few exceptions, the image outlasts the words. Fred Bernard was correct when he wrote in 1927, "A picture is worth ten thousand words."[83] Especially in oral speech, words are spoken and gone. For this reason, preachers intentionally use words which present pictures—metaphors, parables, and stories rich with visual power. On the other side of preaching, listeners visualize what they hear, perhaps like Rembrandt's little artist in *Christ Preaching* or, in most cases, in their imaginations.

Not long ago, I was handed a sheet of paper filled from edge to edge with visualizations of one of my sermons. The listener had attended a workshop encouraging such picturing of a sermon's moves as a way of expressing personal responses to the sermon. I was amazed at what I saw, especially my illustrations visually portrayed. It was certainly more than I had imagined in presenting the sermon, revealing the work of the Spirit accompanying my words as well as the role of the listener in completing the dialogue of a sermon. What's more, it showed how words beg for pictures. Visualization has become a strong tool not only in listening to sermons but also in Bible reading and prayer. The result is a visual journal of one's spiritual disciplines. Connie Denninger, a strong advocate for visualization, has said:

> The use of images, sketchnotes, and markings becomes the way we "inwardly digest" either a sermon, devotional reading, or time spent in His Word. This becomes a signal of movement from only head to heart

83 This is the actual quote using "ten thousand" instead of the popular "thousand" in Fred R. Barnard, *Printers' Ink,* 10 March 1927. See *The Yale Book of Quotations*, ed. Fred R. Shapiro, (New Haven, CT: Yale University Press, 2006).

> knowledge. The "what does this mean" becomes tangible with processes that help us to slow down, pay attention and deal with distractions in our full-speed ahead digital world.[84]

Rembrandt's little boy doodling on the ground while Christ preaches again comes to mind.

The use of image in preaching, though, is not always a move from words to image. Often we move from image to words. We bring an image into our preaching and interpret that image with words. Even if they can view the image as we preach, we may still have something to say about the image. Art has a long history of being followed up with words. The name for this practice is ekphrasis (Greek, *ek*, from; *phrasis*, explanation or description). It sets a picture to words. The words might be poetry or prose or perhaps a story or a simple explanation of the image. If words beg for images, sometimes images beg for words. So the apostle Paul speaking on Mars Hill in Athens points to sculptures of Greek deities, quotes Greek poetry, and then has even more to say. From Homer through Keats and Shelley to Marianne Moore and W. H. Auden, the chasm between image and word has been bridged.[85] So poet John Keats contemplates the images and figures on an urn and writes "Ode on a Grecian Urn," which closes with these words:

> When old age shall this generation waste,
> Thou shalt remain, in midst of other woe
> Than ours, a friend to man, to whom thou sayst,
> "Beauty is truth, truth beauty,"—that is all
> Ye know on earth, and all ye need to know.

So a preacher introduces George Frederick Watts' painting *Hope*[86] into the sermon because the text speaks of hope that cannot be seen (Rom 8:25). The figure in the painting, hope personified, is blindfolded. Tattered and weary, she leans in to hear the music of a single remaining string on her harp. The preacher brings words to this image to describe faith in Jesus Christ as the substance of our hope, fed by the enduring music of the word. The sermon moves from words to image and back to words again. The interplay of word and image will go on still again with added import in the listener's imagination.

84 Connie Denninger in a conversation. For resources and activities, see the work of Visual Faith Ministry at https://www.visualfaithmin.org

85 *Transforming Vision: Writers on Art*. ed. Edward Hirsch, (Boston: Little Brown and Company, 1994), 10–11. The book exemplifies ekphrastic writing as writers respond to works of art at the Art Institute of Chicago.

86 George Frederick Watts, *Hope* (1885, Watts Gallery).

George Frederick Watts,
Hope (Second Version), ca. 1885,
Watts Gallery, London, England
SEE PLATE F FOR FULL-COLOR IMAGE

Preaching as a rhetorical (oral) enterprise is constantly at work moving from word to image and from image to word. It was that way with the prophets. When the prophets spoke, they announced not only what they had heard but also what they had seen. Amos had his locusts, fire, plumb line (Am 7), and summer fruit (Am 8). Jeremiah had his almond branch and boiling pot (Jer 1) and a visit to a pottery house (Jer 18). Isaiah imported images of a mountain (Is 2), a child (Is 7), a stubborn root (Is 11) and desert springs (Is 35) to engage his listeners in the prophetic word. In each case, the prophets had more to say because of the images, and the listeners had more to imagine and remember.

THE USE OF IMAGES IN PREACHING

The use of images in preaching is not without its challenges. The preacher in some cases will use words to plant an image in the hearer's imagination and then more words to address its meaning for the sermon. This may entail simply describing the image, perhaps an art piece, in detail without actually showing the image itself. This can be done effectively, yet it can also end up sounding like trying too hard to describe a sunset or a baby's face. "A picture is worth ten thousand words." In a time when screens seem inseparable from life, listeners may find it difficult to endure the sometimes inadequate plodding of words in a sermon. Some preachers gladly affirm the projecting of visual images in sermons; some do not. Those who do not may feel that the images intrude on the spoken word. Still, their preaching, if it is truly textual, will include the images within a text, winsomely recaptured in their words. Preachers eager to show the images explicit or implied in a text have the option of placing the image in the service folder or on a screen. Care must be given to the copyright protecting some images.

What follows is a survey of several ways to use images in preaching.

Textual Images.

Many texts carry their own images, gifting preachers with strong visual elements for their sermons. These textual images flash across the imagination of listeners even as the text is read. Some are as plain as everyday life and appear in groups of images—a sack of salt, a city on a hill, a burning lamp in the darkness (Mt 5:13–16). Other images wait to be broken open. What is the pearl of great price (Mt 13:45)? How is God's kingdom like leaven in a jar of flour (Mt 13:33)? These are pictures begging for more words, the preacher's words based on the Scriptures. With these images we practice ekphrastic speech, bringing new words not just to a text but to textual images. Such images are also frequent in the narrative of Acts, in the letters of the New Testament, and in the apocalyptic visions of Revelation. Sometimes the images are hidden in metaphors waiting to be unwrapped with more words, as with redemption or atonement. At other times the images are extraordinary and hidden, as in Revelation, begging to be interpreted with more words. Sometimes, as with the stars and lampstands in Revelation 1, the text itself breaks open the image when the glorified Christ says: "As for the mystery of the seven stars which you saw in my right hand, and the seven golden lampstands, the seven stars are the angels of the seven churches, and the seven lampstands are the seven churches" (Rv 1:20). All these images have one thing in common: they are in the biblical text. Because the words of the Scriptures were inspired as oral literature, that is, as writings meant to be read aloud, they often create images in the imagination of those who hear. Not just the words of the Bible but also the images carried by those words are inspired and ready for use in preaching.

Images Imported to Tell the Textual Story and Its Meaning.

Preachers may also use images from outside the written word of the Scriptures. Among them are artistic depictions of scenes from biblical stories and events. We import them because they help tell the biblical story and its meanings. Expressionist painter Max Beckmann, for example, paints the prodigal son in one work as lost in loose living and in another draws him as lost in a herd of pigs. In the second image the runaway is almost indistinguishable from the pigs.[87]

Max Beckmann,
The Prodigal Son Among Swine (Der Verlorene Sohn unter den Schweinen), 1918,
Museum of Modern Art, New York, New York

SEE PLATE G FOR FULL-COLOR IMAGE

The same story's climax is depicted in the beloved painting by Rembrandt, *The Return of the Prodigal Son*.[88] Here the forgiving father embraces his repentant son. Presenting this painting and its many nuances in a sermon on Jesus's parable brings forward the deep, human emotions of the reunion of father and son. Not to be ignored is the older son who stands to the side, troubled by the homecoming. The story, after all, was told for the sake of those who would not welcome sinners. The preacher may reference Rembrandt's own life. Has he painted himself as the prodigal? The father draws the son to himself with strong and gentle hands. It was Dutch priest Henri Nouwen who had spent time at the Hermitage viewing the painting and then put his meditative thoughts in his book, *The Return of the Prodigal Son: A Story of Homecoming*. At one point in the book he considers the hands of the father. He sees those hands as the true center of the painting where the light is concentrated.

87 Max Beckmann, *The Prodigal Son ('Der verlorene Sohn')* [1949, Sprengel Museum, Hannover); Max Beckmann, *The Prodigal Son Among Swine (Der Verlorene Sohn unter den Schweinen)*, 1918).

88 Rembrandt van Rijn, *The Return of the Prodigal Son*, 1669, Hermitage Museum, St. Petersburg, Russia.

> From the moment I first saw [the painting], I felt drawn to those hands. I did not fully understand why. But gradually over the years I have come to know those hands. They have held me from the hour of my conception. . . They have protected me in times of danger and consoled me in times of grief. They have waved me good-bye and always welcomed me back. Those hands are God's hands.[89]

Rembrandt van Rijn,
The Return of the Prodigal Son, 1668,
Hermitage Museum,
St. Petersburg, Russia
SEE PLATE H FOR FULL-COLOR IMAGE

This is ekphrasis at its best—words added to image, careful words, affective words, bringing meaning not just to the image but to the biblical story. If visual depictions of biblical stories help listeners to process a sermon text, they also help the preacher get underneath that text to its meanings and import. Settings vary. Again, preachers may simply describe the work of art, knowing listeners will go to the internet later to view it for themselves. Or they may place the art on a screen or in print in the service folder, observing copyright protection.

Images Imported for Hearer Depiction.

Every sermon in some way seeks to depict the life of the hearer, before and after the gospel move. Much of our preaching is exposé. We show the listeners what their lives in this text look like. The law of God

89 Henri Nouwen, *The Return of the Prodigal Son: A Story of Homecoming* (New York: Doubleday, 1992)

Pablo Picasso,
The Weeping Woman, 1937,
Tate Museum, London, England

SEE PLATE 1 FOR FULL-COLOR IMAGE

shows us our sin. Life under law can certainly be depicted with just words, but it can be enhanced with an image of what the words look like. If, for example, the preacher is addressing the reality of suffering in the Christian life, perhaps from a text in Job or in 1 Peter, Picasso's *The Weeping Woman*[90] may be referenced or shown. Picasso painted the emotions of suffering onto the face of the woman in 1937 during the Spanish Civil War following the bombing of Guernica by the German Luftwaffe. Picasso's mother had written him from Barcelona that the smoke from the burning city had made her eyes water. The dark button-like eyes, the dropped jaw, the purple tears, the clutched handkerchief, and the colors of the woman's face all contribute to a startling and affective portrayal of human suffering. The painting shows what suffering looks like, its shock and agony. Picasso's woman in tears may have at first been received as a tragic victim of wartime horrors, but today she comes to us as the face of human suffering in any setting.

At other times we will use art in our preaching to show our hearers their lives as blessed by God. As the gospel unfolds in the Christian life, we experience flashes of light, unexpected wisdom, and love. This is life under the gospel. It is rich with surprise and grace. Most texts take us there in some way or we work to get our hearers there. In art we can show them what the blessed life, the enlightened life (Jn 1:9), looks like.

90 Picasso, *The Weeping Woman* (1937, Tate Museum). See https://arthive.com/pablopicasso/works/196424~Weeping_woman.

A painting by Edward Hopper comes to mind, *Pennsylvania Coal Town*.[91] Typical of Hopper are the themes of loneliness, light, and shadow in the painting. A man, perhaps a coal miner, rakes his lawn at the side of his house. Shadows frame his singular encounter with a blazing light. We do not see the source of the light, but he does. It holds him entranced. What a contrast from the darkness of the mines! What a moment of epiphany. The mystery of the light holds us. We would like to see what he sees. We wonder what difference the light will make for him. Will it be transforming? The gospel light of Jesus Christ shines in the darkness, and we will not be the same again.

Hearer depiction constitutes much of the language in a sermon. Preachers attempt to shed light on the hearer's experience both before and after the text. Using art provides a crucial reflection (Greek, mimesis) of both these worlds of experience.

Images Imported for Affect.

Often a painting serves no greater purpose in a sermon than to capture the mood of a text. The image gives us the heart of a sermon without the language. We can feel the emotions of the text. Certainly *The Weeping Woman* does that. It's one thing to talk about shock and awe; it is another to see it. Such is the case with Norwegian artist Edvard Munch's, *The Scream*.[92] Munch depicted *The Scream* in five different versions, four in color and one in black and white. The most colorful depiction came in 1895 inscribed with Munch's own note:

> I was walking along the road with two friends. The Sun was setting—
> The Sky turned a bloody red
> And I felt a whiff of Melancholy—I stood
> Still, deathly tired—over the blue-black
> Fjord and City hung Blood and Tongues of Fire
> My Friends walked on—I remained behind—
> shivering with Anxiety—I felt the great Scream in Nature
> E.M.

The foreground figure in the *The Scream* looks hardly human as he or she is overwhelmed by a scream impacted by creation itself. A blood-red sky participates in the scream's shock and awe. Yet the two

91 Edward Hopper, *Pennsylvania Coal Town* (1947, Youngstown, OH: Butler Institute of American Art). See https://www.wikiart.org/en/edward-hopper/pennsylvania-coal-town.

92 Edvard Munch, *The Scream* (1895). For a discussion of the painting and other versions of *The Scream*, see https://www.thoughtco.com/the-scream-by-edvard-munch-182890. A testimony of *The Scream's* significance came in 2012 when the 1895 painting sold at auction for $119,922,500.

companions in the background seem unaffected. Do they even hear the scream? This is a personal scream; one perhaps Munch himself has felt. We know the actual place where the scream may have been heard. It overlooks a fjord not far from Oslo. Munch's sister was a resident of an asylum not far from there. Also nearby was an animal slaughterhouse. Munch knew depression and despair and the deafening shrieks and the utter loneliness they bring. One cannot look at *The Scream* without thinking of the lectionary text, Romans 8:18–25, in which the apostle Paul writes that the whole creation and we ourselves groan inwardly as we await redemption. A sermon on hope has this painting to show what life without hope looks like. At the same time, the painting depicts how isolated we can become in our despair, as Munch's companions walk on, oblivious to the scream. Another lectionary text would be served well by this painting, Galatians 6:1–10, 14–18, where Paul writes, "Bear one another's burdens and so fulfill the law of Christ" (Gal 6:2).

Another well-known lectionary text, Philippians 2:5–11, is a Passion (Palm) Sunday pericope. The text focuses on the Christ-like attitude of humility. The preacher may point people to the prince astride his horse in Frank Dicksee's romantic painting, *The Two Crowns*.[93]

Frank Dicksee,
The Two Crowns, 1900,
Tate Museum, London, England
Photo: Tate
SEE PLATE K FOR FULL-COLOR IMAGE

93 Frank Dicksee, *The Two Crowns* (1900; London, Tate Museum). See https://www.tate.org.uk/art/artworks/dicksee-the-two-crowns-n01839.

All is pomp and flourish, cheers and triumph for the crowned prince. Banners unfurl. Courtly women drop petals of flowers at his feet. His is the procession of a triumphant hero. Yet it all stems from the artist's masterful use of misdirection. As we look closer, we see that the prince's face at the center of the painting is turned to the upper right-hand corner. He looks transfixed, paused, even humbled at what he sees up and away from him. He is transfixed by a crucifix on which Christ is crowned as well, but with thorns. We wonder how this image of Christ will change the prince. Has the thorn-crowned Christ humbled him? "Have this mind among yourselves, which is yours in Christ Jesus . . . he humbled himself and became obedient to death, even death on a cross" (Phil 2:5, 8). How different these two processions, that of the prince and that of the Passion Sunday Savior! How different the crowns! The painting makes humility not merely a thought, but a Christ-centered emotion.

It's amazing how a certain work of art can carry the mood of a text and sermon, so much so that it needs little explanation. It stands on its own to carry the textual ambiance. Take, for example, Van Gogh's *The Raising of Lazarus (after Rembrandt)*[94] depicting the text from John 1:1–45, a lectionary reading in Lent.

Vincent van Gogh, *The Raising of Lazarus (after Rembrandt),* 1890,
Van Gogh Museum, Amsterdam, The Netherlands (Vincent van Gogh Foundation)
SEE PLATE L FOR FULL-COLOR IMAGE

94 Vincent van Gogh, *The Raising of Lazarus (after Rembrandt)* [1890, Van Gogh Museum, Amsterdam (Vincent van Gogh Foundation)]. See https://www.vangoghmuseum.nl/en/collection/s0169V1962.

Much is missing in Van Gogh's painting of the raising of Lazarus, most notably Jesus, who is central in Rembrandt's version of the miracle. There we see the moment of the miracle with the raised hand of Jesus. What Van Gogh gives us is the utter amazement of Mary at what has happened, her wonder, her unexpected joy. Both she and Martha are on their knees. The painting is bathed in yellow, one of Van Gogh's favorite colors, especially in the last years of his life. The yellows give the whole scene the aura of divine presence, joy, and hope fulfilled. Van Gogh has given us our response to the miracle. The sun itself testifies to the glory of the moment. If you look closely at the Lazarus figure, he has a red beard and looks a lot like the artist himself. Van Gogh would die a few months later in 1890. Simply placing the painting before one's listeners captures for them the affective impact of Jesus's miracle.

Images Imported for Their Light.

Some artwork comes into preaching simply as illustration. An image may simply shed light on a truth. Say one is preaching on Psalm 46:10, "Be still and know that I am God." The sermon will call listeners to slow down and rest in prayer. To show them what it looks like, the preacher describes *The Angelus*[95] by French painter Jean François Millet

Jean Francois Millet, *The Angelus*, 1857-1859,
Musée d'Orsay, Paris, France
SEE PLATE M FOR FULL-COLOR IMAGE

95 Jean Francois Millet, *The Angelus* (1857–1859, Musée d'Orsay, Paris, France).

The artist grew up as a peasant, and the scene recalls the prayer traditionally spoken three times a day by those who worked the fields. The prayer, known as the Angelus, focused on the annunciation and the incarnation. Here at sunset the work is ended. The church bells summon all to evening prayer, and there is rest. The couple has set their tools aside. Stillness and reverence fill the frame. In the stillness there is God. How do we find such moments today? What must we set aside if we are truly to rest? Again, the preacher uses the painting to slow down, pause, to contemplate our need to rest in God. Another text served well by Millet's *The Angelus* is Jesus calling the weary and burdened to rest in him (Mt 11:25–30).

Images Imported for Their Own Story.

Sometimes a piece of art is included in preaching because it carries a story related to the text. One such piece is *The Goldfinch*[96] by Dutch artist Carel Fabritius who, like Vermeer, called Delft home. Fabritius painted *The Goldfinch* in 1654, revealing the colorful, captured bird chained to its perch against a stark white wall. His little painting is like much Dutch art of this period—the ordinary, the mundane, and even the boring. On its own, the image illustrates the tragic boredom of being bound with no hope of release.

In Donna Tartt's novel *The Goldfinch*, a thirteen-year-old boy steals the seventeenth-century painting when a bomb explodes at New York's Metropolitan Museum of Art. The boy's mother dies in the explosion. The novel takes it from there. The true story behind the painting, though, is no less tragic. For the artist Fabritius, the year he painted the very ordinary shackled goldfinch was the same year he died. Fabritius perished in a massive explosion in Delft. In the heart of Delft, ninety-thousand pounds of gunpowder exploded when someone tragically struck a match. Egbert van der Poel's painting *A View of Delft After the Explosion of 1654*[97] vividly depicts a devastated city center under a sky of cloud and smoke. Suddenly the ordinary, even the beautifully ordinary, turns dark and tragic. The story behind the painting becomes a depiction of how fragile we are (Ps 90:12), how we do not know the day or the hour of the bridegroom's arrival (Mt 25:13), and how we must work while it is day before the night comes (Jn 9:4).

The preacher does not need a degree in art education to make use of the visual arts in sermons. What is needed, though, is a commitment to visualize sermonic language and moves for the hearer. This commitment parallels the preacher's intentional, ongoing familiarity with the

96 Carel Fabritius, *The Goldfinch* (1654; Mauritshuis, The Hague, The Netherlands).

97 Egbert van der Poel, *A View of Delft After the Explosion of 1654* (1654; The National Gallery, London).

culture's literature (news, novels, poetry, films, and plays) in order to bring to a sermon an engaging narrative appropriate to the biblical text. Just as preachers read intentionally to enhance their communication, they will visit art museums and page through art books to become acquainted with pieces of art which illuminate their text or depict their hearers' lives. These images will serve both law and gospel, trouble and grace.

CHAPTER V
Preaching the Beautiful Christ

For generations preachers have inscribed on their pulpits, the request of a few ancient Greeks, "Sir, we wish to see Jesus" (Jn 12:20). As John records the incident, Philip took their request to Andrew, and together the two disciples went and told Jesus himself. Rather strangely, we are never informed that these Greeks actually saw Jesus in person. News of their interest prompted Jesus to tell Philip and Andrew that the time had come for him to "be glorified" (Jn 12:23). By that he meant that it was time for him to be lifted up on the cross. As often happens in John's gospel, an event is associated with something Jesus said. So perhaps with these interested Greeks in mind, Jesus makes clear what being his disciple entails: "If anyone serves me, he must follow me; and where I am, there will my servant be also. If anyone serves me, the Father will honor him" (Jn 12:26).

Helping people see Jesus is what preachers do. Christ is at the center of our preaching (1 Cor 1:23; Col 1:28). If listeners are to see the beauty of God in our preaching, it will be because they have in some way seen Jesus. "For in him all the fullness of God was pleased to dwell" (Col 1:19). We who preach Christ rely on the imagination of our hearers to present a picture of Christ. Usually that picture is not a still portrait but an action shot of Jesus doing something—teaching, healing, walking on water, and so on. In our description of an action of Jesus, we will not usually say something like: "Then Jesus took those big carpenter hands and brushed his long hair away from his dark eyes and said . . ." We leave the imaging of Jesus to the hearers, each of whom has a distinctive working image of Christ. For some that image has been fed by films portraying the life and passion of Jesus. Actors like Max von Sydow, Jeffrey Hunter, and Jim Caviezel have contributed to generations of imaging Christ. Pictures of Jesus seen in childhood, perhaps from Sunday school, linger in our memories. Some preachers place images of Jesus on a screen to help people "see" Jesus. No doubt most of the images we work with fall short of the likely dark-skinned, Semitic rabbi of the gospels. It's safe to say that if the incarnate Jesus were suddenly to appear before us, we would not recognize him.

Certainly the glorified Christ John saw on Patmos (Rv 1) is hardly the Christ we expect to see.

I grew up in a German-Lutheran church on the south side of Chicago. Founded in 1884, the church became a welcoming community for the third wave of German immigrants coming to America. In the apse at the front of the church, hovering above the altar, was a life-sized sculpture of Jesus Christ modeled after Bertel Thorvaldsen's (1797–1838) famous *Christus* sculpture in Denmark.[98] The sculpture shows a welcoming Jesus, raised from the dead and present to console all who need him. As a child, when my pastor preached, this is the Jesus I saw—a young, bearded, strong man with eyes cast downward toward me, arms extended, and lips slightly parted as if to say, "Come to me . . ." (Mt 11:28). How could there be any other image of Christ in my imagination? To this day, Thorvaldsen's risen, welcoming *Christus* is how I see Jesus when I prepare and preach a sermon. This is the Christ who welcomes all, the Christ of immigrants and exiles, the Christ who is, in every sense, my home. After many years, I am amazed at the power of this particular image to capture for me the major aspects of who Jesus is and what Jesus does.

Over two millennia the church's imaging of Christ has been a story of transitions. If Christology is at the center of our preaching, perhaps the development of the church's artistic depiction of Christ holds some import for how we present Christ sermonically. Our imaging of Christ in preaching is clearly most influenced by the texts from which we preach. If we seek an historical Jesus there is no more reliable record than the Scriptures. The Jesus of the Bible is primarily a storied Jesus, whom we know episodically by his words and actions. We get an event and often Jesus's words to go with that event, and along the way, we get another sighting of Jesus. Certain events, like the incarnation, the crucifixion, and the resurrection stand out on the landscape of these Jesus stories. Our Christology is so impacted by these events that they shape the creeds we confess as Christians. Add to this the various scriptural names we have for Jesus (Son of Man, Son of God, Lord, Christ/Messiah, etc.) and we have plenty from which to build an answer in our preaching to Jesus's own engaging question, "Who do you say that I am?" (Mt 16:15). What we may forget, though, is the imaging that goes on in our listener's imagination. In the stories we tell and in the names we have for Jesus, what do they see? Whom do they see? What does he look like? Tracking the

98 The sculpture was originally commissioned for the Christiansborg Castle Church, but a copy was placed in the Church of Our Lady, Copenhagen, Denmark for its consecration in 1829 and the final marble sculpture remained there. Showing Christ as a resurrected savior rather than suffering on the cross was quite revolutionary at the time. See https://mavcor.yale.edu/conversations/object-narratives/bertel-thorvaldsen-christus-christ.

PLATE A • See page 20 for image reference

Claude Monet, *Stacks of Wheat (End of Summer)*, 1890-1891,
Art Institute of Chicago, Chicago, Illinois

PLATE B • See page 20 for image reference

Claude Monet, *Stacks of Wheat (Sunset, Snow Effect)*, 1890-1891,
Art Institute of Chicago, Chicago, Illinois

PLATE C • See page 36 for image reference

Andrei Rublev, *The Trinity*, 1425-1427,
Tretyakov Gallery, Moscow, Russia

PLATE D • See page 42 for image reference

Lucas Cranach, *Luther Preaching, Altarpiece*, 1547, St. Mary's Church, Wittenberg, Germany

PLATE E

See page 49 for image reference

Michelangelo Caravaggio, *The Supper at Emmaus,* 1601, The National Gallery, London, England

PLATE F • See page 68 for image reference

George Frederick Watts, *Hope (Second Version)*, ca. 1885,
Watts Gallery, London, England

PLATE G • See page 70 for image reference

Max Beckmann, *The Prodigal Son Among Swine (Der Verlorene Sohn unter den Schweinen)*, 1918, Museum of Modern Art, New York, New York © 2021 Artists Rights Society (ARS), New York Photo Credit: Digital Image © The Museum of Modern Art/Licensed by SCALA / Art Resource, New York, New York

PLATE H • See page 71 for image reference

Rembrandt van Rijn, *The Return of the Prodigal Son*, 1668, Hermitage Museum, St. Petersburg, Russia

PLATE I • See page 72 for image reference

Pablo Picasso, *The Weeping Woman*, 1937, Tate Museum, London, England

Photo: Tate

PLATE K • See page 74 for image reference

Frank Dicksee, *The Two Crowns*, 1900,
Tate Museum, London, England
Photo: Tate

PLATE L

See page 75 for image reference

Vincent van Gogh, *The Raising of Lazarus (after Rembrandt,* 1890, Van Gogh Museum, Amsterdam, The Netherlands (Vincent van Gogh Foundation)

PLATE M

See page 76 for image reference

Jean Francois Millet,
The Angelus, 1857-1859,
Musée d'Orsay,
Paris, France

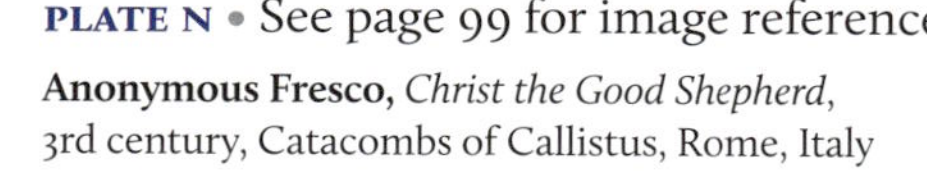

PLATE N • See page 99 for image reference

Anonymous Fresco, *Christ the Good Shepherd*, 3rd century, Catacombs of Callistus, Rome, Italy

PLATE O • See page 101 for image reference

Anonymous Icon, *Christus Pantocrator*, 6th century, Monastery of St. Catherine, Sinai, Egypt

PLATE P

See page 105 for image reference

Matthias Grünewald,
The Crucifixion, from
The Altarpiece at Isenheim,
1512-1516,
Musée Unterlinden,
Colmar, France

PLATE Q • See page 109 for image reference

Francisco de Zurbarán, *Christ on the Cross*, ca. 1630,
Museo Nacional Thyssen-Bornemisza, Madrid, Spain

PLATE R • See page 128 for image reference

Rembrandt van Rijn, *Simeon's Song of Praise*, 1631,
The Mauritshuis, The Hague, The Netherlands

PLATE S • See page 130 for image reference

Rembrandt van Rijn, *Simeon's Song of Praise*, 1669, Nationalmuseum, Stockholm, Sweden

PLATE T • See page 141 for image reference

Michelangelo Caravaggio, *The Calling of St. Matthew*, 1599-1600, San Luigi dei Francesi, Rome

church's depiction of the storied and named Christ may shed light on our own imaging of Christ in preaching.

GRAFFITI AND THE STORIED, IMPERIAL CHRIST

In the first centuries of Christianity, one rarely saw a visual depiction of Christ. His names were depicted cryptically in the ICHTHUS acronym, giving us the first letters of the Greek words, "Jesus Christ, Son of God, Savior." In the catacombs one sees the CHI RHO, the first two Greek letters of the name Christus. They bear a subtle cross when superimposed. The face of Christ, though, is not depicted in these early graffitied signs and symbols. No doubt the influence of Judaism's disdain for graven images of God played in here. Irenaeus, Clement of Alexandria, Lactantius, and Eusebius of Caesarea all disapproved of portraying Jesus visually. Canon 36 of the Synod of Elvira (ca. 306) reads, "Pictures are not to be placed in churches, so that they do not become objects of worship and adoration" (Latin, "Placuit picturas in ecclesia esse non debere, ne quod colitur et adoratur in parietibus depingatur").[99]

The original problem with portraying Jesus Christ was his two natures; he is both human and divine. How does one capture that? The two natures of Christ also present a huge challenge in portraying him in the texts we preach. You can see the struggle addressed in the illustrated Bibles, where Christ is consistently shown with a halo or corona at his head. (The halo does not appear until around 400.) Where our Christology in preaching is concerned, showing both the humanity and divinity of Christ is crucial. Overwhelmingly, in preaching today Jesus appears more human than divine. Even when preaching on texts recording his miracles, some preachers may depict Jesus as a human miracle worker rather than the Son of God who "manifested his glory" (Jn 2:11). We lean toward his humanity.

In the director's guide for his musical *Godspell*, Stephen Schwartz wrote this description for the character Jesus: "Must be the most charismatic individual in the cast. High energy, charming, funny, gentle but with strength. He is the sort of person others instinctively follow."[100] Not a bad appraisal of Jesus from the human side, but hardly adequate for a genuine portrayal of the fully divine and human Christ of the gospels. We still struggle in the arts—our preaching included—with the two natures of Christ.

99 Alfred William Winterslow Dale, *The Synod of Elvira and Christian Life in the Fourth Century* (Macmillan, 1882).

100 Stephen Schwartz, *Godspell Script Notes and Revisions by Stephen Schwartz 1999*. See http://www.oocities.org/cugodspell/scriptnotes.html.

Also, apart from the subtle, symbolic instances mentioned above, the cross is virtually absent in the first three centuries of Christian art. This no doubt reflected the shame attached to crucifixion across the Roman empire. Notable here is one of the earliest depictions of the crucified Christ—a mockery of Christians and of Christ. Originally carved on a wall of the training academy in the imperial palace at Rome, *The Alexamenos Graffito* shows a young man raising his hand in a gesture of worship toward a donkey-headed figure on a cross. The accompanying Greek text reads "Alexamenos worships his God."[101] The image portrays the "folly" of the gospel of a crucified Christ in the mind of an ancient Gentile (1 Cor 1:23). This pre-Constantine graffiti (dated as early as AD 200) points to the perceived oxymoronic practice of Christians worshiping a god who rides on a donkey to his death on a cross.

For today's Christian preacher this graffiti presents the offense of the cross in a pagan culture. When a culture is distant from the witness and stories of the Bible, the cross makes little sense. The Christian faith begins to sound and feel like a butcher-shop religion, with too much blood and slaughter. A lack of understanding or even ridicule may accompany our gospel proclamation. Why did Jesus have to die? And why did he have to die like that? The meaning of the cross can be lost in our preaching if we assume every listener understands its woes and its graces. We have not really preached the cross until we have presented its ugliness and shame, especially when it has the Son of God looking like an ass to those not Christian. *The Alexamenos Graffito* is a crucial image for preachers who recognize that we present Christ in a pre-Christian culture, parallel in many ways to the first centuries of the church.

If, apart from ridicule, the crucified Christ was rarely depicted, how did artists portray him? A third-century image of Christ shows him as a young shepherd with a lamb across his shoulders.

The fresco was painted on the ceiling of the catacomb of Callistus, a large burial site in Rome.[102] Clearly this depiction of Christ expresses the care and sacrifice of Jesus, the "good shepherd" who lays down his life for the flock (Jn 10:11). He will leave the ninety-nine behind to chase after the one (Lk 15:1–7). There is more here, though. As one looks closely at the young shepherd, he has the familiar, unbearded face of a Roman god, resembling depictions of Apollo. The iconic image of such a divine figure with a calf or lamb on his shoulders was well-known across the empire. Early

101 *The Alexamenos Graffito* was discovered in excavations of Palatine Hill in 1857. It can be seen at the Palatine Museum in Rome. See http://www.judaism-and-rome.org/alexamenos-graffito for an understanding of the graffiti as both anti-Christian and anti-Jewish.

102 See http://www.vatican.va/roman_curia/pontifical_commissions/archeo/inglese/documents/rc_com_archeo_doc_20011010_cataccrist_en.html#Pastore

Anonymous Fresco,
Christ the Good Shepherd, 3rd century,
Catacombs of Callistus, Rome, Italy
SEE PLATE N FOR FULL-COLOR IMAGE

Christians took this familiar secular image and, as we have seen before, broke it open with new christological meaning. Jesus is not just a human being who cares, but the Lord who shepherds his sheep (Ps 23:1).

In the same catacomb, another third-century fresco depicts Jesus raising his friend Lazarus from the dead.[103] Again, images of Christ were rare in these first centuries of Christianity. When he was depicted, he was often shown performing a miracle. This one shows him as young, with short hair, and a god-like face. A similar image of Christ from the same period appears on the wall of a baptistery in an ancient house church in Syria. The fresco shows Jesus healing a paralyzed man who, having picked up his cot, walks away whole.[104] Early Christians highly prized the memory of Jesus's miracles. As they buried their dead and baptized their living, they imagined Christ actively facing off with sickness and death and winning the battle. When they looked for hope, they found it in the supernatural power of Christ. They never lived far from the stories of the gospels. As the stories shaped their imaging of Jesus, they gradually found ways to show both his humanity and his divinity. All of this speaks to the need for preachers to present the Christ of the biblical text as informed by the Christology of the entire biblical witness.

103 See http://cojs.org/earliest-known-depiction-of-lazarus-callistus-catacombs-rome-3rd-century-ce/

104 See https://silouanthompson.net/2008/11/healing-of-the-paralytic-dura-europos/

As early Christians buried their loved ones in hidden caves, their comfort often came in recalling and preserving artistically the mighty acts of Jesus Christ in his state of exaltation. These "signs" (Jn 2:11) of Christ captured his divinity with all the wonder of seeing God invading earth with healing and hope. At funerals today preachers present not only a compassionate Christ who weeps with the grieving but also a victorious Christ who has power over sickness and death.

The Edict of Milan (313) by Emperors Constantine in the West and Licinius in the East, brought Christianity and its art out of the shadows. By the late-fourth century, a fresco from the catacomb of Commodilla in Rome depicts Jesus with long hair and a beard.[105] Not lost on art historians is how this and other early portrayals have Jesus resembling pagan depictions of the Greek god Zeus or the Roman counterpart Jupiter. Jesus takes on the look of an emperor and, at the same time, a sage philosopher.

One of the oldest surviving icons was discovered at St. Catherine's Monastery, Mt. Sinai, in the 1950s. Dating from 600 the icon *Christus Pantocrator* shows Christ posed and dressed in purple as an emperor with his hand raised in blessing.[106]

He carries a book, marked with a cross, perhaps the gospels. Stunning here, are the two sides of the face of Christ. To the viewer's left is a younger and very human face, to the right an older and godlike face. The eyes are also different. This early image of Christ reoccurs throughout history, presenting a ruling, powerful, imperial Christ.

In the east, Jesus was consistently portrayed as bearded. In the west, however, the clean-shaven, Apollo-like image persisted even to the time of Michelangelo's *Last Judgment* in the Sistine Chapel. Frescoes and icons on wood panels presented a regal, enthroned Christ.[107] One such depiction of Christ in Ravenna, dated after 500, presents Christ as a cross-wielding warrior king in battle dress, crushing the head of Satan.[108]

Again, in the early iconic portrayals of Jesus, artists strove to show him as both human and divine. They also clearly broke open familiar images of emperors and gods in their portrayal of Christ as regal and divine.

105 See http://diglib.library.vanderbilt.edu/act-imagelink.pl?RC=49950

106 See http://projects.leadr.msu.edu/medievalart/exhibits/show/iconography_of_christ/christ_pantocrator.

107 A good example of Christ as Roman emperor is the mosaic in the apse of Santa Pudenziana Church in Rome. See https://www.khanacademy.org/humanities/medieval-world/early-christian1/a/santa-pudenziana.

108 See https://en.wikipedia.org/wiki/Depiction_of_Jesus#/media/File:Christ_treading_the_beasts_-_Chapel_of_Saint_Andrew_-_Ravenna_2016.jpg.

Anonymous Icon,
Christus Pantocrator, 6th century,
Monastery of St. Catherine, Sinai, Egypt
SEE PLATE O FOR FULL-COLOR IMAGE

They built on what they knew. They adapted imperial and religious portraiture for their images of Christ.

Depicting Christ visually continued to bring its challenges to the church. Especially in the east, in the eighth and ninth centuries, the church was rocked by the iconoclast controversy. Opponents objected to the use of icons or images as objects of worship or veneration. Icons were destroyed, and artists were tortured. After decades of sometimes violent division, the Seventh Ecumenical Council (787) affirmed the use of icons as material symbols, like the image of the cross, opening us to God. Shortly thereafter, in 815, a council again forbade the use of icons. During this period, St. John of Damascus, supporting the use of icons, wrote: "Through the icons of Christ we contemplate His bodily form, His miracles, and His sufferings, and we are sanctified."[109] Finally, in 843 the Council of Constantinople reinstated the use of icons in the church. The Eastern Orthodox Church still celebrates this decision on the first Sunday of Great Lent with the Feast of Orthodoxy.

109 Quoted in "The History and Symbolism of Icons" at https://www.monasteryicons.com/product/The-History-and-Symbolism-of-Iconography/did-you-know.

Icons have maintained their place in Christian worship and devotions. As icons on our laptop screens link us to sites and programs, Christian icons are designed to link us to the greater presence of Christ and all that he brings. They have been aptly described as windows to heaven or doorways to the sacred. The craft and care iconographers give to their art is amazing. They do not depict Christ in the natural world as other artists but present him in a spiritual world as if in eternity. Standardized appearance, the symbolic depiction of clothing, and a familiar use of line and color all usher the viewer into a heavenly, spiritual order, ripe for prayer and contemplation.

The creation of an icon is rich with meaning. In the Eastern church, icons are painted or "written" on carefully shaped wood, symbolizing both the Tree of Life and the cross. A linen cloth protects the wood and recalls the burial cloth of Jesus. Coats of gesso made from rabbit-skin glue and chemists' chalk are applied over the linen, symbolizing the life of Christ. Here is one description of the techniques used by iconographers and the meanings behind them:

> The iconographer cleans, smoothes, and prepares the gesso to receive the holy image, much as we prepare ourselves to bear the image of Christ. The board is indented so that the edges appear raised. The center part of the wood board is shallower than the rest and is called *covcheg*, which is Russian for "coffin." The image is placed inside this shallow space. It is etched into the gesso. A thin layer of clay bole (a mixture of clay and hide glue) is applied to the areas of the icon that will be gilded with gold leaf. The clay represents our physical nature. To apply gold, the iconographer breathes on the clay bole to vaporize it and immediately places the gold leaf on the damp area. This process symbolizes the Spirit and reminds us of the act of creation and the breath of life. The gold itself symbolizes divine light and heaven. Icons often have gold backgrounds because the viewer is gazing at someone in heaven. The image is painted with a mixture of egg yolk, pure water, vinegar, and natural pigments. Many layers are applied, each with their own color symbolism.[110]

Striking is the reverence given to the creation of an icon. Just as significant is the strong awareness of providing a prayerful path into the presence of Christ. Such sensitivity transfers well to the creation of a sermon. The sermon too is a doorway to the sacred, opening us to the holy, wondrous, and mysterious Christ. Approaching a sermon as an icon reminds preachers

110 "Icons as Religious Art" at: https://www.loyolapress.com/our-catholic-faith/family/catholic-teens/religious-art/icons-as-religious-art.

that we are always pointing beyond our words to someone greater and eternal. Like icons, sermons stir the heart to prayer. The breath behind the preacher's spoken words, like the Spirit's first breath of creation, comes with light and life. Sermons are iconic. They are doorways into the sacred, often using familiar language and images but taking listeners into a new order, to the Christ we know and the Christ we have yet to know fully.

THE CHRIST OF THE CROSS

When the image of the cross finally appeared in the first millennium of Christianity, it was not presented as an instrument of extreme torture and suffering but as a symbol, sometimes incorporated into an anchor as a sign of hope. It carried the weight of the victory of empire and emperor. "In this sign conquer." Christ was depicted on the cross but not in a suffering posture. The earliest known depiction of Christ on the cross in the context of his Passion comes with a small fifth-century ivory plaque.[111] Designed for the lid of an ivory coffin, it is one of four panels carved about 420 in Rome. The first shows Jesus bearing his cross uprightly as Pilate washes his hands and a servant points to Peter, who denies Christ. The second is the crucifixion plaque. Jesus is shown on the cross in an upright position, bearing no marks of suffering. He is identified as a king. His cross stands victorious in contrast to the tree from which Judas hangs, his coins spilling out at its base. As a sign of hope, a bird and her young reach toward the cross—a symbol of life and hope. The third plaque depicts the resurrection, the fourth the risen Christ appearing to his disciples and sending them to witness. Absent is the suffering Christ.[112]

Similarly, in *The Road to Calvary,* a sixth-century mosaic at the basilica of Sant' Apollinare Nuova in Ravenna, the procession to the crucifixion shows no sign of Jesus's suffering.[113] Jesus goes to Calvary looking like a king, with no wounds or crown of thorns, but a halo. His cross is carried effortlessly with one hand by Simon, who seems to be his page. The cross here is raised more as an imperial standard than a medium of execution.

The suffering Christ of the cross began to appear more frequently in the church's art at the same time two spiritual giants influenced Christian thought and piety: Bernard of Clairvaux (1090–1153) and Francis of Assisi (1182–1226). Both were gifted preachers. Bernard served as the founding

111 See https://www.worthpoint.com/worthopedia/replica-5th-century-ivory-casket-492729218.

112 For further discussion of this piece see Neil MacGregor, *Seeing Salvation: Images of Christ in Art* (New Haven and London, Yale University Press, 2000), 124. The plaque is held by the British Museum. See https://www.bmimages.com/preview.asp?image=00034960001.

113 Ibid.

Benedictine abbot of Clairvaux Abbey in Burgundy, France. He was perhaps the most influential preacher of the first half of the twelfth century. He served as a counselor to popes and was commissioned by Pope Eugenius III to preach recruiting sermons for the doomed Second Crusade. His personal piety and contemplative writings on the suffering love of Christ are probably best known via the hymn, "O Sacred Head Now Wounded." The hymn is based on the seventh stanza of Bernard's seven-stanza poem, "Salve Mundi Salutare," contemplating the head of Christ as he suffers on the cross. Each stanza of the poem focuses on a different part of Christ's suffering body, his feet, knees, hands, side, breast, heart, and head. Not surprisingly, Bernard is credited with having said, "What we love we shall grow to resemble."

Francis of Assisi, Italy, who founded what would become known as the Franciscan order, followed a very human Jesus. He found in the suffering, crucified Christ a personal compassion toward Jesus and toward all who suffer. Compassion for those who suffer, he found, only enhanced his compassion for Christ. His preaching was simple, practical, and popular. He could preach in as many as five villages a day. Eyewitness reports say that in 1224 Francis received the stigmata, like the five wounds of Christ on the cross. Among many well-known sayings from St. Francis, including his prayers, he gave us this: "My dear son, be patient, because the weaknesses of the body are given to us in this world by God for the salvation of the soul. So they are of great merit when they are borne patiently."[114]

About a century after Francis, the Black Death came to Italy from Asia and spread across Europe. Between 1346 and 1351 the plague likely destroyed over half of Europe's population with a death toll of over fifty million.[115] The plague was present somewhere in Europe every year between 1346 and 1671.[116] Suffering surrounded Christians. The crucified Christ was the Christ who brought comfort to the suffering masses. Seeing him suffering assured them that he knew and understood their suffering. They could readily have compassion for the one crucified. Their contemplation of his image on the cross brought comfort and hope.

Artists' renderings of the crucifixion in northern Europe in the early sixteenth-century presented valuable tools for the preacher. These paintings, woodcuts, and engravings intentionally evoked the emotion, compassion, and identification of the viewer. Artists were striving to create

114 St. Francis of Assisi, *The Little Flowers of St. Francis of Assisi.*

115 Ole J. Benedictow, "The Black Death: The Greatest Catastrophe Ever" History Today vol. 55 no. 3 (March 2005) See http://www.historytoday.com/ole-j-benedictow/black-death-greatest-catastrophe-ever.

116 Stephen Porter, *The Great Plague* (Gloucestershire, UK: Amberley Publishing, 2009), 25.

a fellowship of suffering reminiscent of the apostle Paul's "that I may know him . . . and may share in his sufferings" (Phil 3:10).

Matthias Grünewald, *The Crucifixion,* from *The Altarpiece at Isenheim,* 1512-1516, Musée Unterlinden, Colmar, France
SEE PLATE P FOR FULL-COLOR IMAGE

Matthias Grünewald's *The Crucifixion*[117] is strongly representative of the focus on the suffering Jesus in northern Renaissance art. Grünewald painted the scene as part of an elaborate altarpiece for the hospital chapel at Saint Antony's Monastery in Isenheim, near Alsace, France. Here, Antonine monks cared for lepers, plague victims, and those suffering from St. Antony's Fire and ergotism, both vicious skin diseases. Grünewald's crucified Christ, perhaps more than any other painting, reveals the excruciating brutality associated with crucifixion. Beyond this, though, Grünewald has also given us a suffering Christ who bears on his body the very marks of the skin diseases known and addressed in Isenheim. Isaiah's words come to mind: "Surely he has borne our griefs and carried our sorrows; yet we esteemed him stricken, smitten by God, and afflicted" (Is 53:4).

117 Painted between 1512–1516, the piece has been disassembled and is exhibited beautifully at the Musée Unterlinden at Colmar in the Alcase region of France. See https://www.musee-unterlinden.com/en/home/.

Grünewald places Mary to the suffering Savior's right, her hands clasped in prayer as she faints into the apostle John's arms. At the foot of the cross, Mary Magdalene pleads, also with her hands clasped. To Jesus's left, John the Baptist, with an oversized finger, points to Christ. Clearly John's finger is meant to draw the worshiper's eye to the suffering Savior. John carries the words of the prophets. Floating near him in blood-red letters are his own words, "He must increase, but I must decrease" (Jn 3:30). At John's feet is a lamb bearing a cross. Blood pours from the lamb's heart into a chalice. Those cared for by the monks of St. Antony at Isenheim could not escape that Jesus carried to the cross not only their sins but also their infirmities.

Grünewald's moving depiction of the cross challenges preachers to present a fully human Jesus, calling listeners to join his fellowship of suffering (Phil 3:10). His theology of the cross tells the crucifixion narrative, but it also presents a suffering Savior so compelling as to take on the aspects of devotion, worship, and vocation. This is not a generic or jeweled cross but one deeply personal, hauntingly familiar, and communal, rich with themes of service, sacrifice, and compassion.

A study of three crucifixion woodcuts and engravings by Albrecht Dürer (1471–1528) reveals the artist's various approaches in depicting the cross.[118] Each in its own way emphasizes a very human Christ and the emotions surrounding his suffering and death. Dürer's *Crucifixion,* from *The Large Passion*[119] (cut in 1498) presents the crucified Christ surrounded by the characters of the Passion narrative. It is a crowded composition. Mary, the other women, and John all look away, recalling Isaiah's words describing the suffering servant "as one from whom men hide their faces" (Is 53:3). To Jesus's left is a mounted centurion carrying out the execution and one of the religious leaders hurling insults. In the upper corners of the woodcut, the sun and moon bear witness to the cosmic event depicted in the scenery and dress of Dürer's own time and place. The body of Jesus is upright on the cross, muscles strained. His head is crowned with thorns and radiates the light of his divinity. Apart from his five wounds, his body bears no marks of a brutal beating or flogging. Angels catch the blood from Jesus's wounds in chalices. Dürer is telling the story of the crucifixion and its significance

118 Dr. James Romaine has shown this subtle but significant development in Dürer's woodcuts and engravings of the crucifixion. See "Albrecht Dürer: The Crucifixion" (https://www.youtube.com/watch?v=9GVjpxy70hc).

119 Dürer's *Large Passion* was published in 1511 as a folio-format devotional book, consisting of a title page depicting the Mocking of Christ and eleven large woodcuts illustrating the narrative of Christ's Passion. The images were accompanied in Latin devotional verses by Benedictus Chelidonius (c. 1456–1521), a Benedictine monk from Nuremberg. See https://www.metmuseum.org/art/collection/search/387727.

with little drama or emotion apart from a kneeling or perhaps collapsed Mary who dominates the bottom left corner of the painting.

In Dürer's *Crucifixion,* from *The Small Passion,*[120] (cut in 1509), the characters of the Passion are present, but the cross dominates the space in

Albrecht Dürer, *The Crucifixion,* from *The Small Passion*, ca. 1509, Metropolitan Museum of Art, New York, New York

120 Dürer's *Small Passion* was a portable devotional book of thirty-eight pages published in 1511. Benedictus Chelidonius again provided a shorter set of Latin verses to accompany the images. See: https://www.artic.edu/artworks/75052/the-small-woodcut-passion.

a simpler scene without the angels. The figures are arranged in a way that the viewer cannot help but be confronted by the crucified Christ. There is no identifiable setting for the scene as in the *Large Passion* crucifixion. Most significantly, the figures reveal deep emotions, such as the tears of Mary and the other women. John's hands are raised toward Jesus on the cross, and Mary Magdalene kisses Jesus's feet. Dürer's composition encourages the viewer to enter the scene rather than to view it from the outside. There is room for devotion here and deep emotion. Dürer goes beyond just telling the story. He encourages meditation, prayer, and an emotional response.

A third depiction of the crucifixion comes with Dürer's *The Crucifixion* (1511), from *The Engraved Passion*.[121] The composition here is simpler, still with Christ on the cross and Mary and John on either side. The other women kneel and pray in the background. There is no collapsed Mary here, though, and no John with hands raised. Both are in a posture of contemplation and prayer. Their emotional response will not take the viewer's eyes from the cross. Rather they invite a Christ-centered meditation focused on the meaning of his suffering and death. Yet again, Dürer has composed a different crucifixion scene, one very personal, inviting a response of quiet worship and contemplation.

Artists of the Renaissance understood the crucifixion to be more than a story to be learned and told. An unforgettable painting by Italian artist Francisco Ribalta (1565–1628), *Saint Francis Embracing the Crucified Christ* (also known as *The Crucifixion*), carries the theme of communion with the suffering Christ to the extreme.[122] Ribalta depicted Francis embracing Christ on the cross, his lips near Jesus's wounded side as if ready to drink his blood. Jesus has removed the crown of thorns from his own head and extends it to place it on the head of Francis, inviting him to join in the suffering. Visible on the right foot of Francis is one of the stigmata. An angel brings a laurel wreath for the head of Christ while other angels provide music for the occasion. At the foot of the cross are seven defeated beasts, signifying victory over evil and the deadly sins. This engraved print (rather than woodcut) allowed for a fresh and dynamic contrast of light and darkness, only heightening the drama of the moment. Again, devotion, emotion, and deep meaning come with this depiction of

121 *The Engraved Passion* included a cover page and fifteen copper engravings. The popular series was published repeatedly in Northern Europe throughout the sixteenth and seventeenth centuries and was used for devotional and teaching purposes. See: https://www.wga.hu/html_m/d/durer/2/13/3/11crucif.html.

122 Painted about 1620, *Saint Francis Embracing the Crucified Christ*, also known as *The Crucifixion*, is held by Museo de Bellas Artes de Valencia in Valencia, Spain. See: https://www.wikiart.org/en/bartolome-esteban-murillo/saint-francis-of-assisi-embracing-the-crucified-christ.

the cross. In her commentary on this painting, Gabriele Finaldi includes a hymn by religious poet Miguel Sanchez, a contemporary of Ribalta, capturing well the two pleadings of Ribalta's *The Crucifixion*:

> Innocent Lamb of God
> Bathed in your blood
> Which frees the world of sin,
> From the strong wood
> Upon which you hang, with open arms
> You implore me to embrace you. . .
> Before your pure and royal soul
> Departs to save me,
> Turn your tender eyes to look upon me.[123]

This very personal meditation on the cross captures in words what artists strove for in their composition and figures at the cross.

The Council of Trent in the mid-sixteenth century encouraged reducing the crowded depiction of Golgotha. It became common in the sixteenth and seventeenth centuries, especially in northern Europe, to see artists showing Christ on the cross, alone with his suffering. Absent were the accompanying figures of Mary, John, and others. One such painting is Francisco de Zurbarán's *Christ on the Cross* (ca. 1630).[124]

Francisco de Zurbarán,
Christ on the Cross, ca. 1630,
Museo Nacional Thyssen-Bornemisza,
Madrid, Spain

SEE PLATE Q FOR FULL-COLOR IMAGE

123 Quoted in Gabriele Finaldi, *The Image of Christ* (London: The National Gallery, 2000), 122.

124 Francisco de Zurbarán, *Christ on the Cross,* c. 1630, (Museo Nacional Thyssen-Bornemisza, Madrid, Spain).

Among the purest of crucifixion scenes, the painting simply shows Christ suspended on the cross, bathed in light against a deep black background, looking and speaking heavenward from the cross. Perhaps the moment Zurbarán captures is Jesus's prayer for forgiveness on behalf of those who crucified him. If so, poignantly, he is also praying for the one viewing the painting. Clearly, there is no desire here to capture the narrative with all its characters in all its fullness. Rather, Zurbarán is giving us an image for meditation and prayer. He is not so much teaching us a story as he is showing us what ultimate love, salvation, and sacrifice look like in Christ. He is inviting us into all that Christ offers in his sacrifice.

A similar painting, Diego Velázquez's *Christ Crucified* (also 1632), uses the same stark darkness and light effects on a solitary figure, only here it is Christ at the moment of death.[125] Such depictions of a lone, suffering Christ on the cross became more and more common and continue today as images in worship places across the world. Clearly depictions of the cross developed from a conspicuous absence in early Christian art to a dominate subject of Renaissance artists.

Artists of the crucifixion have much to teach those who preach the crucified Christ. Perhaps a good place to start is with a sermon by Martin Luther. In 1519 Martin Luther was preparing his lectures on Galatians as well as researching canon law for his Leipzig debate with John Eck. He was also preparing a Good Friday sermon which would be printed as a pamphlet and distributed across Europe.[126] The sermon was a treatise on how Christians rightly meditate on the Passion of Christ. He begins by identifying three wrong approaches to such meditation: a venting of anger for the Jews who asked for his crucifixion; an emphasis on the blessings and advantages that come to those who spend hours contemplating the Passion; and a sentimental compassion toward the suffering Jesus that never moves beyond weeping for Christ to weeping in repentance for our own sins. The latter no doubt stems from the very popular use of paintings and prints in Lent for lengthy meditations, focused more on having pity and compassion for the suffering Savior than any real change in the Christian heart. In fact the last line of Luther's sermon reads: "We have transformed the essence (of the Passion) into semblance and painted our meditations on Christ's passion on walls and made them into letters."

The sermon challenges Christians to meditate on the Passion with more than pity toward Christ. Luther calls them to see how their own sins

125 Diego Velázquez, *Christ Crucified*, 1632 (Museo de Prado, Madrid, Spain).

126 *LW* 42, 3-14.

put Christ on the cross. He moves on to proclaim the love of the Father in sending Jesus there. As expected, Luther "law/gospels" the Passion. In meditating on the Passion of Christ, we realize first that Jesus is on the cross because of our sins. Luther writes:

> You must get this thought through your head and not doubt that you are the one who is torturing Christ thus, for your sins have surely wrought this . . . Therefore, when you see the nails piercing Christ's hands, you can be certain that it is your work. When you behold his crown of thorns, you may rest assured that these are your evil thoughts, etc. . . . For every nail that pierces Christ, more than one hundred thousand should in justice pierce you, yes, they should prick you forever and ever more painfully! When Christ is tortured by nails penetrating his hands and feet, you should eternally suffer the pain they inflict and the pain of even more cruel nails, which will in truth be the lot of those who do not avail themselves of Christ's passion.[127]

This is highly visual language, creating images in the hearers' minds. There is no stopping with the law, though. As we meditate on the suffering Christ, Luther says, repentance and faith move us to an overwhelming awareness and confidence in God's love for us.

> You must no longer contemplate the suffering of Christ (for this has already done its work and terrified you), but pass beyond that and see his friendly heart and how this heart beats with such love for you that it impels him to bear with pain your conscience and your sin. Then your heart will be filled with love for him, and the confidence of your faith will be strengthened. Now continue and rise beyond Christ's heart to God's heart and you will see that Christ would not have shown this love for you if God in his eternal love had not wanted this, for Christ's love for you is due to his obedience to God.[128]

Then the gospel unfolds in the Christian life. As Luther puts it, "After your heart has thus become firm in Christ, and love, not fear of pain, has made you a foe of sin, then Christ's passion must from that day on become a pattern for your entire life." In the sanctified Christian life, Luther shows how the Christ of the Passion and the cross empowers us to endure our own suffering, to do the difficult thing, and to overcome temptation, a spirit of vengeance, grief, and fear. He calls his listeners to an active response to their meditation on the Passion.

127 *LW* 42, 9.

128 *LW* 42, 13.

Luther has clearly structured a very Lutheran sermon! Notice, though, that he is not just passing on information or telling a story. His language is simple, vivid, and rich with imagination. He asks his listeners to see not only Christ on the cross but also their own fears, temptations, guilt, and struggles. His listeners had plenty of opportunities to visualize the suffering, crucified Christ before they came for worship. He now taps into those images and speaks with the pathos of one who has found love, not just suffering, in the figure on the cross. He speaks with the ethos of a preacher for whom Christ's passion and cross have become a pattern for his own life. What's more, he does what artists do—he invites his listeners into a scene they already have in their heads, and he opens it up with meaning and impact.

The crucifixion would continue to be a subject of visual artists for succeeding generations. Whatever the school of art, the cross has been there. Most artists since the Renaissance, even if not Christian, have shown an appreciation for the classical portrayal of the crucifixion. Some have even based their portrayal of the cross on the works of past classical artists, but in a new style. As the cross has loomed large on the landscape of Christian preaching, so it has continued as a subject in the schools of art over the last two centuries. Modern art has not walked away from the cross but embraced it. A "Modern Gallery of the Cross" especially for preachers would easily include depictions of the crucifixion by impressionists Edgar Degas and Paul Gaughin; expressionists Georges Rouault and Emil Nolde; and surrealists/symbolists Pablo Picasso, Marc Chagall, Francis Bacon, and Salvadore Dali.[129] Each of these artists goes beyond realism to capture the pathos, shock, and relational impact of Jesus's suffering and death. Each can provide inspiration for the preacher in preparing a sermon and a fresh look and perspective on the crucifixion for sermon listeners.

THE RISEN, ASCENDED, AND RETURNING CHRIST

Five works depicting the post-resurrection Christ carry significance especially for preachers. Again, the preacher may place the images before the congregation on a screen or service folder or may simply describe

129 Edgar Degas, *The Crucifixion (after Mantegna)*, 1861 (Musée des Beaux-Arts de Lyon, Lyon, France); Paul Gauguin, *The Yellow Christ* ,1889 (Art Institute of Chicago); Georges Rouault, *Crucifixion*, 1937 (Minneapolis Institute of Arts); Emil Nolde, *The Life of Christ, Center Panel, Crucifixion*, 1912 (The Nolde Foundation, Seebüll, Germany); Marc Chagall, *White Crucifixion*, 1938 (Art Institute of Chicago); Pablo Picasso, *The Crucifixion,* 1930 (Musée Picasso, Paris, France); Francis Bacon, *Crucifixion*, 1933 (Murderme Collection, London, England); and Salvadore Dali, *Christ of St. John of the Cross,* (based on a drawing by a sixteenth-century Spanish monk), 1951 (Kelvingrove Art Gallery and Museum, Glasgow, Scotland) and *Corpus Hypercubus*, 1954 (Metropolitan Museum of Art, New York, NY).

the images to the listeners.[130] The first piece is the *Altarpiece at Isenheim* by Matthias Grünewald and *The Resurrection* panel.[131] Few artists have attempted to depict the moment of the resurrection. After all, there were no recorded witnesses of that moment. The same Christ Grünewald depicts so horribly in *The Crucifixion* panel and then for burial in another panel now beams with transcendent light, piercing the darkness of death. His guards lie shocked and scattered by the explosion. The heavy sepulcher stone is behind him. He shines like the sun as in his transfiguration, and his white burial linens rise with him, flowing now with regal colors up from his tomb. Grünewald has captured the glory of the moment of Jesus's resurrection. The use of light and color dazzle the eye. He gives us a Christ rarely seen and too rarely heard in sermons, the Christ of glory, displaying his five wounds, breaking through the bonds of death, the Christ fully human, yet radiantly divine.

Titian's *Noli Me Tangere (Do Not Touch Me)* gives us Mary Magdalene with her risen Lord outside the unseen sepulcher as she realizes that it is he who stands before her.[132] She had mistaken him for the gardener. Titian has placed a gardener's tool in Jesus's right hand. Mary kneels before him, leaning on her jar of ointment, reaching to touch him. In John's gospel, Jesus says, "Do not cling to me, for I have not yet ascended to the Father" (Jn 20:17). Titian masterfully has Jesus pulling back, using his burial cloth as a shield, but at the same time leaning toward Mary. A tree's gentle leaning has the viewer leaning in with Mary toward Jesus. On Jesus's side of the painting all is green and growing with a flock of sheep pasturing in the distance. Titian has captured the deep mutual love between Jesus and his disciple as well as the change the resurrection brought to that relationship. Again the humanity and divinity of the risen Lord are evident. Neil MacGregor in his *Seeing Salvation* mentions that this was the first "Picture of the Month" brought back for monthly display at The National Gallery in London in 1942, after the museum's entire collection had been moved to Wales for preservation during the bombings of World War II.[133] In the midst of death and destruction, thousands came and reached with Mary for the life the risen Lord brings.

130 For more on these post-resurrection pieces, see MacGregor, *Seeing Salvation: Images of Christ in Art*, 179-193 and Finaldi, *The Image of Christ*, 168–191.

131 Matthias Grünewald, *The Resurrection* from *The Altarpiece at Isenheim*, 1512–1516. Musée Unterlinden at Colmar, Alsace, in France. See https://www.musee-unterlinden.com/en/categorie_oeuvre/the-altarpiece-of-issenheim/.

132 See https://www.nationalgallery.org.uk/paintings/titian-noli-me-tangere.

133 MacGregor, *Seeing Salvation*, 191.

When preaching on John's record of the risen Christ and the doubtful Thomas, preachers can hardly find a more dramatic image than Caravaggio's *The Incredulity of Saint Thomas*.[134] Artists since the sixth century have found this incident in the resurrection narrative worthy of depiction. Though Caravaggio goes beyond the biblical text, which does not indicate that Thomas actually touched Jesus's wounds, his use of darkness, shadow, and light (chiaroscuro) masterfully provides a realistic, three-dimensional view of Christ. The viewer looks in on the scene as much as the other two disciples, perhaps Peter and John. Caravaggio gives us a very human risen Jesus, without halo, bathed in light, guiding Thomas's finger to the wound in his side. The clothing of all the figures, including Jesus, is hardly ethereal, but earthy in color. At a time when a new form of gnosticism emphasized a Christ more spiritualized than corporeal, Caravaggio's affirmation of a bodily resurrection is crucial. It assists the preacher in proclaiming the creedal "resurrection of the body," that of Christ and ours still to come.

Neil MacGregor's commentary on Albrecht Dürer's woodcut, *The Ascension,* from *the Small Passion*, clearly reveals its value to preachers.[135] For centuries, artists chose to depict the ascension of our Lord by simply showing him on the mountain with his disciples or already in the cloud above them. In this little piece, Dürer takes a different perspective. He has us looking upward with Jesus's disciples, and what we see is only the bottom of Jesus's robe and his feet. He rises from the earth attended by a cloud and leaves his footprints behind on the earth. Dürer wants his viewers to look at the ascending Jesus from the perspective of a disciple. MacGregor has an appreciation for the difficulty in depicting such movement on a woodcut and even calls it seemingly "absurd as Christ vanishes from sight like a self-propelled missile."[136] That said, Dürer's perspective draws the viewer into the story. Imagine heads tilted upward in a worship service to see only the hem of Jesus's robe and his feet as he ascends like a rocket! The image brings to a sermon a rare participation in a biblical text.

At a time when eschatology is almost absent from the witness of contemporary preaching, artistic depictions of Christ's return and judgment are especially valuable. Growing up, I can recall being enthralled by a painting on the wall in our church basement depicting the last

134 The painting is exhibited at the Picture Gallery at Park Sanssouci, in Potsdam, Germany. See: https://www.wikiart.org/en/caravaggio/incredulity-of-saint-thomas.

135 MacGregor, *Seeing Salvation*, 192. Albrecht Dürer, *The Ascension,* from *The Small Passion* (ca. 1510), Metropolitan Museum of Art.

136 Ibid.

Albrecht Dürer, *The Ascension,* from *The Small Passion*, ca. 1510, Metropolitan Museum of Art, New York, New York

judgment. Dinners and Christmas bazaars happened in that same room and looming over it all was Christ on his white judgment throne. It was common over the centuries to have such a scene painted on the interior wall of a church. Today it is rare. Perhaps that is why when the received texts for preaching give us Christ returning in judgment, a preacher would do well to turn to an image like Fra Angelica's *The Last Judgment*.[137] Here Christ is seated on his throne attended by Mary and John and the angels and saints in light. His left hand sends those on his left to hell. His right hand sends those on his right to heaven. Hell is depicted as fiery and painful with Satan devouring the damned. To Jesus's right we see an angel ushering the redeemed through a garden, paradise, to a celestial city. The either/or of the judgment is blatant and uncompromised. It is difficult to deconstruct or even discount the image based on Jesus's own words in Matthew 25 and the unified eschatological witness of the Scriptures. At the center of the painting, graves are broken open, signifying the bodily resurrection. The confession of the Nicene Creed is vividly portrayed: "And He will come again with glory to judge the living and the dead, whose kingdom will hand no end" and "I look for the resurrection of the dead and the life of the world to come."[138] This enduring confession becomes less vague in our preaching when visualized by this and other depictions of the last judgment.

CONCLUSION

In this chapter, we have focused on presenting a beautiful Christ in our preaching using artistic images. Preachers have an extensive gallery from which they can visualize the Christ of their text. As we have seen, sometimes the image will simply be there as an enhancement of the text and the preacher's words. At other times, the preacher will want to provide some commentary on the image, pointing to its connections to the unfolding text or to an engaging story behind the image's creator or history. All of it serves as a presentation of Christ that goes beyond speaking and hearing.

In an essay titled "Preaching and Christology," Elizabeth Achtemeier begins by excluding certain approaches to the subject:

> By dealing with Christology and its relationship to preaching, we are dealing with faith's preaching of the good news of Jesus Christ. We are not treating the widespread practice of therapeutic preaching, in which the purpose of the sermon is just to make the congregation feel comfortable and reassured. We are not discussing the preaching of humanistic insights and moves. We are not even dealing with the widespread practice of moralizing. A congregation that is enslaved to sin cannot "just get out there and do good." Above all, in discussing our topic, we are not dealing with the so-called third quest, with the critical hunt for the "real Jesus" to be discovered by historical, sociological, or psychological criticism.[139]

137 Fra Angelica, *The Last Judgment*, 1425–1430 (Museum of San Marco, Florence, Italy). See: https://www.wikiart.org/en/fra-angelico/last-judgment.

138 Nicene Creed, *Lutheran Service Book* (St. Louis: Concordia Publishing House, 2006), 158.

Then what is the focus of christological preaching? With this chapter's emphasis on preaching a beautiful Christ, how does that happen? As Achtemeier puts it, "The witnesses to Jesus Christ . . . and therefore the subjects of New Testament Christology, are indissolubly embedded in a narrative, and faith in Jesus Christ is dependent on that narrative."[140] The narrative of which she writes is the biblical narrative, the grand story of the Bible and all of its sub-plots. Each witness to who Christ is. Achtemeier warns:

> If we begin to dismantle the narratives of the Bible, in all their continuity and diversity, then we have no firm foundation for faith. The Jesus who is separated from the biblical narratives' context ends up a totally unrecognizable figure, unknown to the church and indeed unknowable.[141]

Presenting the Christ of the biblical narratives "in all their continuity and diversity," is what preachers do. We tell stories centered in Christ. These stories give us pictures in our minds and have yielded a treasure lode of immeasurable beauty in the arts. In a real sense, the artists of the church have helped preserve the inspired stories we have in the written text. In helping us visualize Christ in what we read and hear, they have helped us remember the stories, even if our culture has forgotten them. They have helped us tell our stories. Many observers of the contemporary church, Walter Bruegemann among them, has likened this time in the church's history to the time of the exiles in Babylon.[142] That makes it a time when we need to tell our stories well and sing our songs without fear.

Holocaust survivor Elie Wiesel shares an old Hasidic fable that makes the importance of narrative clear.[143] He gives us Rabbi Israel, who, when his people faced misfortune, would go into the forest, light a fire, and pray. Then a miracle would happen, and the misfortune was averted. Many years later, one of Rabbi Israel's disciples, Magid, faced misfortune with his people. He went to the same place in the forest and prayed, "Master of the universe, I do not know how to light the fire, but I can say the prayer." And the miracle was accomplished. Still much later, a third rabbi, Moshe,

139 Elizabeth Achtemeier, "Christology and Preaching," in *Who Do You Say That I Am?* ed. Mark Allan Powell and David R. Bauer, (Louisville, Kentucky: Westminster John Knox, 1999), 264–265.

140 Ibid., 265.

141 Ibid.

142 Walter Brueggemann, *Cadences of Home: Preaching among Exiles* (Louisville: Westminster John Knox, 1997), 1–14.

143 Elie Wiesel, *The Gates of the Forest* (New York: Holt, Rinehart, and Winston, 1966), Preface.

faced trouble with his people and went out to the forest and said, "I do not know how to light the fire, and I do not know the prayer, but I do know the place, and that, I hope, is sufficient." And it was. Finally, so many years later, Rabbi Israel sat in his chair with his head in his hands. As he and his people faced misfortune, he said, "I do not know how to light the fire. I do not know the prayer. I do not even know the way to the forest. All I can do is tell the story, and this must be sufficient. And it was."

Elie Wiesel closed this story with, "God created man because He loves stories."[144] In preaching we present a storied Christ to a storied listener, connecting those stories through language rich with image. Each story has its own beauty, but when connected with the stories of Christ preachers find the sweet spot for which they work, for which they live.

144 Ibid.

CHAPTER VI
The Image-Structured Sermon

Intentional Use of Image

The role played by images in preaching can be ignored but not denied. Whether preachers realize it or not, their words are busy creating images in their listeners' minds. The image intended by the preacher may not always be the same in the listener's imagination since each listener brings a unique pallet and brush to the sermon. Listener images are shaped by experience and memory. People often see what they have seen before. This is true when it comes to seeing Christ in their imagination or seeing their own lives as suggested by the preacher's words. One way to affirm the use of images in a sermon is to simply preach and leave it to the listeners' imaginations to create an image or gallery of images. Occasionally, though, the preacher may be more direct saying, "Close your eyes for a moment. I'd like you to imagine . . ." As dreams invade our restful consciousness with vivid images, so images appear in the restful consciousness of those listening to a sermon.

Suggested here is a more intentional use of image, one by which preachers choose a specific image or images to shape their sermon's structure and moves. The preacher here is actively visualizing the sermon text and its application. The text is still the driving force shaping the sermon, but the preacher intentionally enhances the text by the images the text itself suggests. This makes preaching an art and places the preacher in the company of poets. Now the preacher does not simply provide information or ideas but comes at truth and goodness with a beauty that cannot be denied. Now language will be remembered for the images it creates. Now metaphor and story lead to imagined and actual pictures, and the preacher sounds more like Jesus, whose preaching and teaching piled image upon image.

Peter Jonker in his little book, *Preaching in Pictures: Using Images for Sermons That Connect*, makes a strong argument for this intentional use of image in preaching.[145] He places preachers in the company of not only

145 Peter Jonker, *Preaching in Pictures: Using Images for Sermons That Connect* (Nashville: Abingdon, 2015).

artists and poets but also marketers. What marketers understand is the power of an image to place us into a story. Jonker writes:

> When a good image takes hold of our imagination, it puts us in a story. We see the image and we momentarily imagine ourselves transported out of our present lives—with their worries and troubles—and into a more perfect, more joyful, more fulfilling future.
>
> As preachers these sorts of propulsive, story-creating images are just what we want at the center of our sermons.[146]

Jonkers references Jamie Smith whose books, *Imagining the Kingdom and Desiring the Kingdom*,[147] show how secular marketers engage both imagination and desire. While preachers are at work trying to shape a generation by presenting propositional truths, Smith argues, the other persuaders in the world are going for the heart with images. We in the church often expect ideas to win over passions. Jonkers counters:

> If we want to be effective preachers, we have to understand how modern marketing works, and we must learn to aim our presentations of Christ's love at the heart as well as the head. We must offer images of God's saving work that stand up against the flashy promises offered in that sexy commercial featuring the shiny new car perched on a desert mesa or the hopes inspired by that carefully staged dream kitchen in the pages of the latest home decorating magazine.[148]

For some preachers the idea of "marketing" a text will run directly counter to their intuitive confidence in the word of God to accomplish the purposes for which God sends it (Is 55:11). The word will do what it does, we affirm. Just preach the word. Yet the word itself is replete with images that capture the imagination and desires of its readers and listeners. Other preachers may be uncomfortable with the idea of persuasion as the purpose of preaching, despite that being the goal of classic rhetoric for centuries. Yet the prophets and writings of the Old Testament, the teachings of Jesus, and the letters of the New Testament persuade people into kingdom life via story and metaphor. Our confidence in the scriptural text is not only in its source but also in its pure goodness, truth, and beauty. To object to the use of images in preaching—whether imaginative or actual—echoes the iconoclast controversy which in some ways still haunts the church. Image will appear in our preaching because image appears in the text of the Scriptures.

146 Ibid., 66.

147 James K. A. Smith, *Imagining the Kingdom: How Worship Works* (Grand Rapids: Baker Academic, 2013). James K. A. Smith, *Desiring the Kingdom* (Grand Rapids: Baker Academic, 2009).

148 Jonker, *Preaching in Pictures*, 65.

A SINGLE CONTROLLING IMAGE

As preachers seek a central theme for their sermon, they may also want to search for a central or controlling image.[149] This is approached best by reading a biblical text aloud, noting the various images raised by the text. This requires a contemplative listening to the text for what God gives us to see. As you're reading this, pause for a moment to read aloud or recite the beautiful words of Psalm 23. As you hear yourself say the words, jot down all the images raised by this incomparable lyric. Here are the results of my own textual image inventory: shepherd; green pastures; still waters; paths of righteousness; valley of the shadow of death; rod; staff; banquet table with enemies present; my own anointed head; overflowing cup; house of the Lord. That's eleven images! Individually, each image carries not only significant cognitive truth but, just as importantly, deep beauty and emotional impact. Further, as listeners bring their own experience and needs to these images, their cumulative power is formidable. Still, the preacher may want to ask, "From these images, which one seems to carry the psalm for me this time around?" Just as preachers may choose a single statement as the central thought of a sermon, they may also focus on one of the images throughout the sermon, coming back to it again and again. In Psalm 23, for instance, instead of focusing on the shepherd image, the preacher may choose the banquet table as a controlling image. Clearly, whatever the sermon's controlling image, it must be wedded to the sermon's central theme.

In searching for a controlling image, the preacher may opt for an image outside of the text, yet clearly suggested by the text. Often the images outside the text come from a consideration of hearer depiction. In other words, the preacher is asking, "What images from my listeners' lives are suggested by this text?" So, again using Psalm 23 as our text base, the preacher may find a central thought for the text that says, "With the Lord I am in a safe place." Certainly the text offers several images to match this theme. Here, though, the preacher may begin the sermon asking listeners to consider a safe place they had as a child and to go there in their imaginations. An image of a safe place from the preacher's own experience would be helpful here. The preacher does not ignore the vivid imagery of the text but allows this image of hearer depiction to dominate his sermon.

Another option in seeking a controlling image is to provide an artistic image on a screen or in the service folder carrying the focus of a safe place. Here, rather than imagining, the listeners are given an actual image to

149 See Yonkers, *Preaching in Pictures*, 26–29. Yonkers bases much of his work on Paul Scott Wilson's integration of image into sermon preparation in *The Four Pages of the Sermon* (Nashville: Abingdon, 2018).

contemplate. An obvious choice for a sermon on Psalm 23 would be one of the several photos of ancient graffiti or sculpture in the catacombs depicting Jesus as the good shepherd.[150] A favorite image of artists in the early church, as discussed earlier, shows Jesus as a young Roman, resembling Apollo, carrying a ram on his shoulders. Another choice would be a photo of a child asleep in her father's arms or a car pulled under an overpass during a violent storm.

The use of a single image in preaching is based on the notion that just as one picture is worth ten thousand words, one picture is better than ten. The use of a single image in a sermon may follow one of these alternate structures:[151]

1. Single Image Imagistic.

The preacher uses a single image to launch the sermon and returns to it thematically throughout the sermon to recapture the sermon's central theme.

2. Frame and Refrain Imagistic.

The preacher uses a single image at the start of the sermon and then returns to it at the sermon's close. The image frames the development of the sermon's central thought as a launch and as asummary at the close.

3. Image Delayed Imagistic.

Here the single image is not introduced until the close of the sermon and serves to summarize the sermon's main theme or to recall the major moves of the sermon. Traditionally pastors have used a poem or a hymn for this purpose. In addition to the sermon closing with words, listeners see the sermon in a single closing image.

MULTIPLE IMAGES

As an alternative to using just a single controlling image, the preacher may use multiple images in a sermon. Here a unifying thread from the text runs through two or more images as each image moves the sermon forward. Preachers who regularly use software to project images on a screen know how their own functional memorization of the sermon can actually be prompted by the image for each successive move.

150 For example, *Jesus as the Good Shepherd*, mid-third century. Mural, S. Callisto catacomb, Rome. See: https://www.bibleodyssey.org/en/tools/image-gallery/s/shepherd-werlin

151 This nomenclature is suggested by David Schmitt in his essay "Sermon Structures" on the Concordia Seminary, St. Louis, MO website link: http://concordiatheology.org/sermon-structs/. For further elaboration, see his article, "Sermon Structures: The Image-based Design" in Concordia Pulpit Resources 12.1 (2001): 5–9.

David Schmitt has suggested the following movements within a sermon using multiple images:[152]

1. Movement within a metaphorical field.

The images may depict the movement from light to darkness or from desert to fertile field, from valley to mountaintop.

2. Typological movement.

Here the images could be the ark of Noah and the baptism of a new Christian. Another might be the bronze snake raised in the desert and Christ lifted on a cross.

3. Dynamic reversal.

Here the images could reveal such radical movement in a text from despair to hope, humility to exaltation, bondage to redemption, or sadness to joy.

4. Development of a theme.

Multiple images here reveal growing aspects of a theme such as discipleship, worship, the presence of Christ, or prayer. In every case, the movement depicted by these multiple images reflects a movement clearly there in the text and pictured for the listener.

CHOOSING AN IMAGE

In choosing an image for use in a sermon, the preacher will want to be sure the image meets the criteria of an effective communication tool. The following questions can be helpful in selecting an image or images for a sermon:

1. Does the image have clear roots in the biblical text or at least an obvious connection to the text?
2. Does the image relate directly to the central thought or theme of the sermon?
3. Is the image appropriate for the listeners? That is, does the image reflect their experience? Will it appeal to most if not all listeners?
4. Is the image memorable?
5. Does the image engage the senses of the listener?
6. Does the image engage the emotions of the listener?
7. Does the image move the sermon forward?

Commenting on the play *Hamlet*, C. S. Lewis wrote, "To interest is the first duty of art; no other excellences will ever begin to compensate for

152 Ibid.

failure in this."[153] A similar commitment to engagement characterizes the beautiful sermon. Both lazy language and lazy imagery are enemies of effective preaching. Just as a preacher's use of cliché or repetitious language can diminish the delivery of law and gospel, so the repeated use of an overly familiar image can detract from a sermon's impact. Preaching as an art entails choosing words and pictures which serve the biblical text and carry a beauty and a power to transform.

153 C. S. Lewis, *Selected Literary Essays*, ed. Walter Hooper, (Cambridge, UK: Cambridge University Press, 1969), 103.

CHAPTER VII
Three Sermons with Commentary

Preaching is learned well by listening to, or as in this case reading, real sermons. In this chapter, three sermons are presented along with commentary as the sermon unfolds. The first sermon was preached to listeners over the radio. The second sermon was preached at the installation of a pastor. The third was preached in a congregation served by the preacher. The sermons were chosen for their affective and aesthetic qualities, hoping to show what a beauty-driven sermon looks like. All three sermons intentionally make use of visual art for beauty's sake and for the sake of strong oral composition. Writing to be heard must be rich with images and the use of the hearer's imagination.

The structure of these sermons reflects the moods and moves of the text itself; they progress simply and logically to make the sermon easy to remember. A good measure of a sermon's structure is whether listeners could re-preach the sermon in their own words after the preacher has finished. No less a measure of a sermon structure is how well the listener knows the text when the sermon has ended. These measures guided the structuring of these sermons.

Ultimately, the beauty of a sermon is carried by the gospel's presentation of a beautiful Christ, beautiful in his presence, his words, his actions, and his love. The beauty of Christ is the single most significant aspect of a sermon's aesthetic quality. Because preachers deal here with an ultimate beauty, their words and images will falter and fail, but sometimes, amazingly, they offer a glimpse into the beauty that is Christ, even without ever using the word, beautiful.

A LONG GOOD-BYE

A Sermon for the Sunday after Christmas
Luke 2:27–32 (ESV)

> And he (Simeon) came in the Spirit into the temple, and when the parents brought in the child Jesus, to do for him according to the custom of the Law, he took him up in his arms and blessed God and said,
>
> "Lord, now you are letting your servant depart in peace,
> according to your word;
>
> for my eyes have seen your salvation
>
> that you have prepared in the presence of all peoples,
>
> a light for revelation to the Gentiles,
> and for glory to your people Israel."

Striking in this well-known text is how it addresses universal ("all peoples") and national ("Israel") themes as well as the very personal presence of Christ ("my eyes") for Simeon. The sermon will zoom from the wide-angle lens of the text to the very personal witness of Simeon. From both views, the preacher aims to present both the beauty of Christ and the beauty of a relationship with him. On the heels of Christmas Day, the sermon encourages a personal encounter with Christ. Two works by Rembrandt embody the twin perspectives on the meaning of Christ's presence—Christ for the world and Christ for the individual. The sermon begins with the textual introduction of Simeon.

The old guy had a lot going for him, this Simeon. Luke tells us that Simeon was "righteous" and "devout"—a good man. He was waiting for "the consolation of Israel," Luke says. That's the language of messianic hope, the prophet Isaiah's language of "Comfort, comfort my people." Simeon was waiting for the promised Messiah who would console God's people in all their sorrows. And if that's not enough, we're told that the Holy Spirit was upon him. The Spirit had promised Simeon that before he died he would see the promised Messiah, "the Lord's Christ." This wise old senior citizen was walking hope. Where he went hope in the Messiah went with him.

The textual story is retold, and Simeon's song explained. Anna, as in the text, is introduced briefly with admiration. The beauty of the moment and of Simeon's song in the life of the hearers are highlighted.

Maybe he had gone there often before, looking at the babies presented by their parents at the temple, wondering if this or that one might be *the* one.

Then one day it happened. Mary and Joseph brought their newborn son Jesus for the appointed ceremonies of purification and presentation, and Simeon knew, this is the one! He stepped in and took Jesus in his arms and blessed God and sang his heart out.

We know his song as a kind of "good-bye" song. It has been sung in the church for centuries at the close of communion services and evening worship. Old Simeon's song says his life is fulfilled because he has seen with his own eyes the salvation of the world. This baby in his arms, he sang, means light for Gentiles and glory for Israel. That takes in everybody. When he finished singing, old Simeon turned to Mary and Joseph and blessed them. He told Mary that the lives of many in Israel would rise or fall on her child. Her child, he said, was a sign, a miracle, that would face opposition. He warned that a sword would pierce Mary's own heart. It would not go easy for Jesus.

An 84-year-old widow was there in the temple, too. Anna had dedicated her life to the Lord. Just then, at the same moment, she began praising and thanking God for this child who would satisfy all who waited for the freedom only the Messiah could bring. And she got the word out that freedom was on the way.

From a simple retelling of the textual story, the sermon now reaches into the life of the hearer. Two perspectives on the person of Christ emerge from the text—that of the larger-world narrative and that of the personal story of Simeon. Two works by Rembrandt embody these perspectives. The images are imported for their affective impact and for the story behind them. I am hoping that the listener will experience in real time both the very grand and the very personal presence of Christ. Since this sermon was first presented on a radio broadcast, I will need to describe each in detail.

The first Rembrandt piece gives us the grandeur of the Christ, the big story behind the tiny baby.

So what do you take from this event? What do you think Luke, the inspired gospel writer, wants us to know? Tradition has always seen Simeon as an old man. That may be, but we should be careful here. This is more than a story about how good and wise senior citizens can be. That may be appealing, especially if you are a senior citizen yourself, but God has more to say here than that. Luke tells this story because it tells us something about Jesus, out of the gate, so to speak, right from the start.

For one thing, Simeon's song places Jesus into a greater story that reaches deep into history, to the heart of God, to the fall into sin in the garden, to the call of Abraham, to the exodus and the prophets, to all of that and all the promises God made and kept along the way. Simeon had been waiting for the consolation of Israel, and now that consolation was in his arms!

Of all the depictions of the presentation of Jesus in the temple, perhaps the best-known are those of Rembrandt, the seventeenth-century Dutch painter. He first painted "Simeon in the Temple" in 1631 when he was just twenty-five years old.

Rembrandt van Rijn, *Simeon's Song of Praise*, 1631,
The Mauritshuis, The Hague, The Netherlands
SEE PLATE R FOR FULL-COLOR IMAGE

One sees already in this early painting the skills of a master, and you can't miss the grandeur and beauty of the temple as he paints it. One senses the big story behind the tiny baby. You can't miss Rembrandt's genius in depicting the grand temple architecture and the many different figures in the temple courts. As you'd expect, the light in the painting radiates from Jesus in Simeon's arms to the whole sprawling space, as if to show us this "light to the Gentiles and the glory of Israel."

You cannot help but sense it—in Luke and in Rembrandt—the bigness of this moment. What God had promised, what God's people had prayed for over many generations, what the whole world needed, whether it knew it or not, here he was in Simeon's arms. The Messiah, the Christ! What we celebrate in this Christmas season is big and grand and rich and cosmic and for everyone. As Simeon sings it, this has been "prepared in the presence of all peoples!" God has come to earth! The whole world is the object of God's love, a love so deep and so wide that God sent Jesus, his Son, to save it, to set it free from sin and death. Simeon sang it. Anna shared it with everyone she met.

The sermon next moves from many to one, from great to small, from the big narrative to this one story—a man holds the Messiah in his arms. Again a later Rembrandt piece shows the humble and personal coming of Christ to Simeon. My intent in using this second, later Rembrandt piece is to help the hearer experience personally the zoom from universal to personal. The story behind the paintings will help to bring this home.

Yet as Luke records the event, we simply can't stay at this global level. As Simeon sings, this all becomes very personal. "Lord, now you are letting your servant depart in peace, according to your word; for *my* eyes have seen your salvation." "My eyes," he says, "My eyes have seen your salvation." For Simeon and Anna, Jesus was not just the Savior of the world; he was their Savior. It was global, but it was also very personal.

It's just as Martin Luther preached it: "The gospel does not merely teach about the history of Christ. No, it enables all who believe it to receive it as their own, which is the way the gospel operates. Of what benefit would it be to me if Christ had been born a thousand times, and it would daily be sung into my ears in a most lovely manner, if I were never to hear that he was born for me and was to be my very own?" That's it. Jesus was born for the whole world, but he was also born for you.

Remember, I mentioned Rembrandt's early painting of Simeon in the temple. Fast forward with me to one of Rembrandt's last paintings, perhaps his very last. The painting was found unfinished in his studio, the day after he died in 1669. It was another depiction of Simeon in the temple. Thirty-eight years had passed since Rembrandt's early painting of the same scene. His life had been a series of gains and losses, good and bad decisions. In his "The Return of the Prodigal Son," he had painted himself as the prodigal son. Now he faced failing health and increasing debt. By this time, both of his wives and all but one of his children had died.

Rembrandt van Rijn,
Simeon's Song of Praise, 1669,
Nationalmuseum,
Stockholm, Sweden
SEE PLATE S FOR FULL-COLOR IMAGE

Here in this painting the grandeur of the temple is gone. Rembrandt does not seek to impress us with his skills. It's just one old man painting another old man, Simeon, who cradles his Savior in his arms. Simeon's eyes are half shut, his wrinkled face bathed in soft light. There is one other nearby figure in the painting, a woman, perhaps Anna, but most commentators believe someone else may have added that figure to the painting later. Perhaps, I can only guess, Rembrandt in his later years caught how deeply personal this was for Simeon and for himself. It is as if history and tradition, prophecies and holy places all fade next to the simple beauty of an old man cradling his Savior.

Having recreated Rembrandt's second painting of the presentation in the imagination of the listeners, I will invite each of them to step into the scene and know the very personal presence of Christ. The language is intentionally affective. Using a Minnesota tradition, "The Minnesota Long Good-Bye," I hope to show how where love is, good-byes can be protracted.

Today, before the Christmas season runs itself out, before the year runs itself out, before your life runs itself out, I invite you step into this scene from God's word. Like Simeon, take the baby in your arms. Look into his eyes and let his little hand grab your finger. Squeeze his little feet. And know that this is the one who grew to be your salvation, the one whose hands and feet were pinned to a cross for you. Let this word, this picture, pierce your heart. This is not just the hope of the world and the hope of a great and long story; this is your hope.

In Minnesota we have a custom known as "the long Minnesota good-bye." It happens when you've been visiting with friends or family and someone says something like, "Maybe we should get going." The conversation continues, though, and continues. We just love being with those we love (or maybe it's so cold outside we don't want to face it). But a quick "bye," wave, or hug just never seems to do it. Minnesotans always give the full send off, walking you to the door, out on the driveway, to your car and maybe even still shouting to you as you start to pull out on the street.

We don't know how long Simeon or Anna lived after this event in the temple. We do not hear from them again in the Scriptures. This event was so significant for them, though, they couldn't just experience it; they had to sing it and praise it and tell it in a sort of long good-bye. Their long good-bye today has reached even us two millennia later, still engaging us, still blessing us.

Two applications follow, one on growing older, the other on the new year ahead. Along the way a little lesson on hope is provided.

It is true that as we grow older, life itself can become a long good-bye. We may face the loss of loved ones and friends, perhaps a lessening sense of significance or productivity. We may contend with health challenges, slowing down, losing control, struggling to remember. In all of that, the Spirit of God gives the grace we need to see Jesus with eyes of faith. The word in all of its beauty gives us pictures like this one—Simeon holding the Christ child. In our faith-driven imagination, as time passes by, we can picture Jesus, and he gives us hope. Time + Faith + Imagination = Hope. Let me say that again: Time + Faith + Imagination = Hope. Where we are and where we will be, Jesus is also, and someday, like Simeon, we will see our Savior Jesus face to face with our own eyes, then in all of his glory.

The end of a year can be a long good-bye too, no matter how old you are. We want more time, more time. We can beat ourselves up over what seems to be an unfinished life. We can live with regrets and guilt. We may worry over what the next year will hold for us. This One, who is our salvation, came to save us and to free us from all of that as well.

The sermon closes with a strong sense of fulfillment in Christ—deeply personal fulfillment. Our greatest questions are answered in him. Our hope for the future is in him. The sermon close is a celebration of what is and what will be for each of us in Christ. Intentionally, I want my hearers to imagine themselves cradling Christ. With cues from Simeon and Rembrandt, this culminating image invites them to step into the textual story and make it their own.

In Jesus we are fulfilled. In Jesus, all the great questions of life are answered. Where did I come from? God created me. Who am I? I am God's child. Why am I here? To give God glory as I love God and my neighbor. Where am I going? To heaven by grace through faith in Jesus.

As this year draws to a close, we take our turn after Simeon. We each hold the baby, and his light, his glory, shines upon us. Here, now, in this child we become people of hope, walking hope, singing hope, witnessing hope. No need for good-byes here, short or long. He will never leave us or forsake us. He is there in the Scriptures. He is there in our baptism. He is there in bis meal of forgiveness. He is there in every word that reconciles or consoles, every act that serves and sacrifices in his name, every faithful witness. His grace is more than sufficient to take us into another year and into a new heaven and a new earth. Just as he did with old Simeon, Jesus gives us peace and pure, grateful, contagious, get-the-news-out joy! May it be so! Amen.

HIM WE PROCLAIM

A Sermon for the Ordination or Installation of a Pastor
Colossians 1:28–29 (ESV)

> Him we proclaim, warning everyone and teaching everyone with all wisdom, that we may present everyone mature in Christ. For this I toil, struggling with all his energy that he powerfully works within me.

> *I chose this text for its focus on Christ as both the subject and strength of the church's proclamation. In the previous sermon, I spent time meditating on the text before moving into application. Here, the sermon will simply follow the moves of the text, beginning and ending with a focus on Christ. Assurance is the affective posture of the preacher. The intentional beauty of the sermon rests primarily, of course, in its Christology and in the cherished relationship between pastor and people.*

Three words, "Him we proclaim," three words in English and three words in the original Greek New Testament. "Him we proclaim." And in that order. "*Him* we proclaim." Not all the versions of the New Testament get that right. "Him" comes first for emphasis. But there it is, "*Him* (Christ) we proclaim." And it is not Christ plus something. It is Christ, just Christ. Christ alone—"*Him* we proclaim."

> *The text provides a grammatical emphasis on the supremacy of Christ in the life of pastor and people. That is celebrated and further defined in what follows. Here, the sermon proclaims the beauty of Christ and the gospel by presenting the Christ event, its benefits, and where one finds them (locality).*

Christ we proclaim. Not the Christ of our own imagination, but the Christ of the gospels, the Christ of the Scriptures! Not Christ, the founder of a religion, but Christ the Son of God! Not Christ the therapist or Christ the humanist or Christ the good teacher, but Jesus Christ, the Savior of the world, who carried our sins to the cross and paved the way to eternal life for us by rising from the dead! That's whom we proclaim. Not some misty, dusty, distant Christ, real and unreal, but the true Christ of the gospels, fully human and fully God. That Christ! Not a Christ so heavenly that he is irrelevant, but a Christ immersed in our lives and making his home in our hearts! Not a Christ so lofty that he is incomprehensible but a Christ as simple and profound as "Jesus loves me, this I know, for the Bible tells me so."

> *Listeners no doubt have questions about their new pastor. The most important question is answered here, striking at the heart of the pastor's identity and ethos. Our pastor, like us, is a sinner redeemed by Christ.*

I know you're wondering about your new pastor. What can you expect? What will it be like? For certain, a seminary education matters, skills matter, personality matters, your pastor's family and experience matter. What matters most, though, is this: your pastor personally believes the good news of forgiveness in Christ and has come to proclaim that good news. I can vouch for that. You can be sure of that. Your pastor is a sinner redeemed by Jesus Christ, a Christian, an authentic follower of Christ. That is where your relationship with your pastor can begin today.

Here, I import an image to help the hearers contemplate the beauty of Christ in the relationship between the pastor and people. The Cranach painting of Luther preaching plants an image in the minds of the listeners, affirming the centrality of Christ in their life together. It is a strong image, familiar to some of the listeners but not to all. I was fortunate to have a screen on which it was displayed. In a smaller sanctuary I would have brought my copy of the painting and held it up in the pulpit.

Almost 500 years ago artist Lucas Cranach painted Martin Luther preaching to his congregation in Wittenberg. On one side of the painting Cranach, a friend of Luther's, gives us the reformer at work in the pulpit. On the other side is the congregation, some more intensely focused on the preacher than others. And at the very center of the painting is Christ on the cross. Luther has one hand on his Bible as he preaches while his other hand points the congregation to the crucified Christ, his linen cloth unfurled like a banner victorious in death and in resurrection. Christ at the center of it all—preacher and people together in Christ. He will be the center of your pastor's preaching. He will be the source of your pastor's authority and love. He will lead your church through his servant, Pastor _____, and all those other servant leaders among you.

The "we" of this text affirms the vocation of every Christian to proclaim Christ in their own spheres of listeners. The pastor may hold the office of public proclaimer on behalf of the congregation, but the work of proclaiming Christ in the world has always belonged to all Christians. Here I try to reveal the proclamation Christ as a team enterprise.

And then there is the word "we." Him *we* proclaim. This is the apostle Paul, the great apostle Paul, but he uses the word "we." Kingdom work was always a team effort for Paul. It is the same for us. So when pastors preach, they preach not only to us, but for us, and with us. It's as if you can say, "What my pastor just said, if I was up there, that's exactly what I would have said, too. That's my proclamation, that's our proclamation. It's what we believe together."

"Him *we* proclaim." Preaching the good news of Jesus is never a one-way enterprise. It's one thing to have a dynamic preacher. It's just as important to have dynamic listeners, people who take time to read the biblical text of a sermon and bring to the sermon their own needs and prayers.

And when the apostle Paul says "we," he is assuming that others will be busy proclaiming Christ as well. Pastors do not have the sole rights to proclamation. Parents will proclaim Christ to their children. Everyday Christians will proclaim Christ to their neighbors, coworkers, and classmates. Truth is, your new pastor needs you if your church is to extend the kingdom. No pastor can do it alone. They depend on the great "we" of the church's proclamation.

The personal story which follows seeks to plant a memorable image in the mind of the listener, capturing the "we" of Christ proclamation. This story taps into the cherished image of shepherd, rich in the history of our faith. It is told here to affirm that pastor/shepherds cannot do the work of proclamation alone. In fact, they may fall very short of the good shepherd.

As a young pastor, my first church in Eugene, Oregon began the practice of a living nativity. Near Christmas, we built a stable, brought in live animals, and for three nights the youth of our church performed a brief pageant. We brought the living nativity idea with us to our church in Edina, Minnesota. We quickly figured out that a living nativity pageant presented on the cold tundra would need to be done even more briefly and with warm coats under the costumes.

Unfortunately, that first year, we had built the fence around the stable too short. Sure enough, on the first night, as the pageant began, one sheep jumped the fence and took off down the road, a frontage road for a major highway. The other three were sure to follow. I shouted out panicked commands for others to chase the three while I confidently exclaimed, "I'll take the lead sheep!" Off we went. I chased that sheep a good half mile up the road and finally took it down in a snow drift. It was one of the best tackles I ever made.

There in the drift I suddenly imagined a picture I had loved since I was a kid—Jesus the good shepherd. I remembered Richard Hook's fine painting and the old catacomb pictures of Jesus carrying a sheep atop his shoulders. So in a flash of confident inspiration, I attempted to lift the sheep to my shoulders. This was the fattest sheep God ever created! Halfway up, I wrenched my back and fell back into the drift, holding on to the sheep's wooly back side.

I was down and couldn't get up. I had to shout for help. Three burly high school football players arrived, found me in the snow, and together the four of us led that sheep home. I will always cherish the muffled applause we received (everyone was wearing gloves) as four lost sheep were brought home to the fold, one-by-one, by a total of twelve different shepherds. I simply couldn't have done it alone. "We" had to do it together. "Him we proclaim."

The sermon is slowly unfolding the text and now comes to the word "proclaim." At various points, the sermon has worked at definition. Here the concept of proclamation is defined, bringing with it the sense of intense precision, passion, and urgency. The definition works with exclusions as well—what proclaiming Christ is not.

And that third word: "Him we *proclaim*." That word, proclaim, in the original New Testament, takes the word for "announce" and intensifies it. It means to announce decisively and precisely; it means to herald significant news in a definite and binding way. It is a deeply intense and urgent word. This kind of proclamation makes no excuses. It is not tentative. It is not wishy washy nor is it deferential to an opposing word. It is clear, definite, passionate, and urgent. It's a word that doesn't dilly-dally or procrastinate or compromise. It is straightforward proclamation of news that transforms lives for eternity.

Many churches today struggle with isolation from their community. Paul's use of "everyone" in the text provides a launch pad for a church's reach not only to its immediate neighborhood but also to its global outreach. Even the small church has the "everyone" mandate.

And notice that this proclamation is not just for ourselves. It's not a weekly pep talk for insiders. Paul goes on to say in verse 28, "warning everyone and teaching everyone with all wisdom, that we may present everyone mature in Christ." Did you catch that? Three times he says "everyone." We warn *everyone*, we teach *everyone*, all with the hope of presenting everyone mature in Christ. "Everyone" doesn't mean a few or some or as many as we can . . . it means everyone, the whole world, because "God so loved *the world* that he gave his one and only Son."

The text also presents the hard work and even agony of leadership in the church. Listeners need to know what their pastor faces and what they face with him—a world not eager to receive the Christ proclamation. The vignette of a little boy against the "whole world" captures this challenge and hopefully leaves a memorable image. The image of this story, like that of the earlier story of the pastor and the sheep, works with humor and grace.

It does not paint the pastor or the people as powerful and successful in the ways of our world but as humble and often struggling servants of a living Lord.

So the proclamation is never meant to be within these walls only. It goes out from this pulpit and this altar to "everyone" in this church's sphere of influence. And that takes work. That means it won't be easy, and it won't be a solo enterprise. So Paul goes on to say, "For this I toil, struggling with all his energy." Paul knew struggles in ministry. Proclaiming Christ put Paul in prison not once but often. The words he uses in verse 29, "toil" and "struggling," are hard words. The original word for struggling here gave us our word "agonizing." Truthfully, your pastor's work is among the most difficult of any profession. There will be times when in prayer for you or in facing times of conflict, he will agonize over his ministry. He will struggle.

Fewer people these days are choosing full-time ministry in the church. The price is high. Add to that the fact that the days are gone when the church's message is eagerly received with open minds and hearts. It takes real work now to be heard, to be given a place at the table, when claims to truth are so quickly rejected. Our day is much like Paul's. It's been described as a pre-Christian era. The world, still loved by God, seems antagonistic to God.

I love the story of the four-year-old who was working with his dad in the garden. Dad was weeding and encouraged his son to help out. Finally, the little guy grabbed a weed and began to pull. He tugged and tugged. He yanked and groaned and yanked again. Finally, the weed gave way. The boy landed on his back with eight pounds of dirt and weed on his chest. Dad smiled and wanting to encourage his son, simply said, "Good job, son. You sure are strong!" The four-year-old answered. "I sure am, Dad!" he said, "I held on to one end of that weed and the whole world had the other end, and I won!"

The close of the sermon, like the text, will return to Christ at the center of our future together as pastor and people. The sermon close will reprise the textual theme.

For the apostle Paul it was all too much for him to do on his own. And today it is the same for pastors and every proclaimer of the gospel. So in verse 29 Paul gives us one of those priceless verses with a surprise pronoun. He writes, "For this I toil, struggling with all his energy that he powerfully works within me." The surprise pronoun? "For this I toil struggling with all *his* energy, which *he* so powerfully works within me." Who is behind that "his?" Whose energy is it? Christ's! Yes, the very one who is the focus of our proclamation is also the source of our energy and strength.

So where we began is where we end. How did T.S. Eliot put it?

> We shall not cease from exploration
> And the end of all our exploring
> Will be to arrive where we started
> And know the place for the first time.[154]

We began with Christ, and that is where we end. We know this place. As you begin your life together as pastor and people, as you commence this great proclamation adventure, Christ will be your energy, Christ will be your strength, and Christ will be your victory. "Him we proclaim." Amen.

154 T. S. Eliot, "Little Gidding," *T. S. Eliot: The Complete Poems and Plays 1909–1950* (Orlando, FL: Harcourt Brace & Company, 1967), 138.

"FOLLOW ME"

A Sermon for the Second Sunday after Pentecost or St. Matthew, Apostle and Evangelist • Matthew 9:9–13(ESV)

> As Jesus passed on from there, he saw a man called Matthew sitting at the tax booth, and he said to him, "Follow me." And he rose and followed him.
>
> And as Jesus reclined at table in the house, behold, many tax collectors and sinners came and were reclining with Jesus and his disciples. And when the Pharisees saw this, they said to his disciples, "Why does your teacher eat with tax collectors and sinners?" But when he heard it, he said, "Those who are well have no need of a physician, but those who are sick. Go and learn what this means: 'I desire mercy, and not sacrifice.' For I came not to call the righteous, but sinners."

The sermon is narrative in character with two personal narratives framing the sermon's textual work. The text evokes personal narratives since this is Matthew's own account of his call to follow Jesus. The opening personal narrative is used to build the contrasting tensions (between awesome and ordinary) that will unfold in the sermon and lie at the core of the beauty of Christ. A core focus of the sermon is how the wonder of grace empowers Jesus's disciples to movement and transformation. The beauty of the sermon is in Christ, his power and truth, his magnetism and mercy, and the change he brings in us.

The other day I had a quick conversation with a fellow I met where I get my hair cut. He had just overheard my conversation with the stylist and had figured out that I was a pastor. We were both on our way out of the shop and he stopped me outside the door and said, "Hey, I'm a Christian." "Great," So am I." I said. He laughed and then he said it: "Awesome!"

He proceeded in about three minutes to tell me his story—how Jesus had changed his life.

"It was like someone turned the faucet on and couldn't turn it off. It was awesome!" he said. Laced throughout his little testimony was that word, awesome.

"Isn't God awesome?" he said.

"Isn't Jesus awesome?" he said.

"Isn't it awesome what God does and how God does it," he said.

He quickly told his story, a before-and-after story of dramatic transformation. "Imagine it," he said, "that God would call someone like me! Awesome!"

He hardly took a breath, this new disciple of Christ, and he was oblivious to the fact that we were standing in the rain the whole time.

I don't use the word, awesome, very much, probably because it has been greatly overused, sometimes for things that aren't really all that awesome. The word, miracle, gets overused, too. Some people use the word, miracle, when they get a good parking place. As someone has said, if miracles happen as often as people say they do, we might as well call them ordinaries. But here was a guy who was so fresh in faith, so overwhelmed by how Jesus Christ had changed his life, he was living with one "awesome" after another.

The call of the apostle and evangelist Matthew is awesome in its own right. If awesome means an encounter with the numinous, if awesome means amazing and dynamic, even transformational, then awesome is all over this story.

Matthew (his real name was Levi) was Jewish and should have been working in the temple. Instead he took up the dishonest work of a tax agent for Rome, doing what they all did, charging people more than he should have, sending Rome what it needed and pocketing the rest for himself. People hated tax agents. We're may not be too crazy about the IRS today, but the people in Jesus's day took it to another level, seeing tax agents as traitors and crooks.

Now Matthew doesn't ever say "awesome," when he tells his story. It's one of the most downplayed matter-of-fact testimonies you'll ever hear. Matthew gives us the story in his own Gospel, using the third person rather than first. As he straightforwardly gives us the facts of the story, we hear about one awesome occurrence after another. It's awesome that Jesus is even talking to a crooked tax agent. It's awesome that it only takes two words from Jesus, "Follow me!" to get Matthew up from his table. It's awesome that the next thing we hear is that Jesus and Matthew and a bunch of people from the dark side are having dinner together at what we can assume is Matthew's house. And it's awesome that when the Pharisees criticize Jesus for having dinner with these contemptible lowlifes, Jesus reminds them that he didn't come for the religiously righteous but for sinners, that he is all about mercy. He didn't come for the spiritually healthy, he says, but for those who know that they are sick and need to be healed. Despite this string of amazing, awesome events, Matthew never once uses the word amazing or awesome. He simply gives us the story as it happened in as simple and unadorned language as possible.

With the textual narrative told, I want the hearers next to visualize the story in Caravaggio's well-known painting. Here, the image is imported to help fill the textual story with meaning. The way the two conversion stories were told (developing the tension between awesome and ordinary) has prepared the hearers to experience the beauty of Caravaggio's envisioning of the Matthew text. After that occurs, the image is then imported to tell its own story, as the brief reference to Caravaggio's life reveals. These two uses (importing the image to tell the textual story and importing the image to tell its own story) work with one another to lead the hearers from text to application. The image was printed on the service folder as a take-home piece and projected on a screen.

Over 400 years ago Renaissance painter Michelangelo Caravaggio was commissioned to paint the call of Matthew for a church in Rome. In his own understated way, as in Matthew's Gospel, Caravaggio's *The Calling of St. Matthew* catches the amazing nature of this event.

Michelangelo Caravaggio, *The Calling of St. Matthew*, 1599-1600, San Luigi dei Francesi, Rome
SEE PLATE T FOR FULL-COLOR IMAGE

On the far right is Jesus with a faint halo around his head. That's probably Simon Peter with Jesus. Jesus has just entered the room and with him this amazing beam of light falls on Matthew, who counts his money with his accountants and young bodyguards. You can see the surprise on Matthew's face and that finger pointing to himself as if he's answering Jesus's "Follow me," with a "You talking to *me*?" It's all understated in the painting but the awesomeness of it is all over the place. Matthew and his friends in their fine clothing, and Jesus and Peter barefoot! And that hand of Jesus following the light to point to Matthew! You can't see it, but Jesus's feet are already turned to head out the door. In a moment, Matthew will stand, get up from the table, and walk out that door behind Jesus of Nazareth. Out of the darkness into the light!

It's no secret that Caravaggio, the painter, was a brawler, a murderer on the run, and a very difficult man. He drank too much and died too young, and in his own life bore witness to what God could do with a sinner. Caravaggio understood Matthew.

The use of the image has prepared the hearers for application. The sermon now offers two applications from the textual story and a clear presentation of the gospel. I want my hearers to see grace at work as well as the necessity for movement as they follow Christ. The beauty of the gospel gives us Jesus, full of grace and truth, someone we can trust to be out front as we follow. Even as application occurs in this sermon, notice how the language contains echoes of earlier images. These echoes continue to bring the hearers back to the beauty of Jesus, experienced in the text and now in life.

So what can you take with you from this story? There is so much here. For one thing, notice the sheer power of grace. Why would Matthew leave a lucrative business to follow a barefooted Jesus into poverty and an unknown future? Grace has to be the answer. The fact that Jesus accepted him as he was, not when he cleaned up his act but while he was steeped in sin, had to astound Matthew. He was hand-picked, and the grace that accepted an outsider like him must have overwhelmed him.

I think it is true—that those new to the faith often express the wonder of grace more than those who have been following Jesus for decades. Perhaps that is the way it is with those who have followed Jesus for years. They live in the wonder of grace every day. Perhaps that's the way it was with Matthew, who writes this account long after he got up from the tax table. Or is there something else? Perhaps the lack of wonder on Matthew's part as he tells his story is there because Matthew's focus is on Christ, not on himself. Maybe for Matthew what matters most here, what lingered years later, was the person of Jesus, his cherished words, and his astounding grace. This brought the wonder, a wonder present with every disciple of Jesus Christ, but felt and expressed by some more than by others.

A second takeaway in this story is the movement of discipleship. Matthew moves. He can't stay at the table counting his money. Jesus taught that it had to be one or the other, God or Money, not both. For us, that means if our faith is alive, there will be movement from darkness to light, from hate to love, from worship to growth, from growth to service. It's not the religiously stagnant whom Jesus affirms; no, they are condemned. Jesus goes for those who have to move and change, even radically. He goes for those who need him most lest they wallow and die in their own righteousness.

Referencing next the 2008 REVEAL study by the Willow Creek Association will hopefully help listeners consider their own movement and growth as Christians. The stages of growth identified in that study reflect over 75,000 surveys from 230 churches. The church I served at the time participated in the survey. A primary discovery of ours was that 10 percent of our worshipers fit into Group One, those who are exploring the faith, believing in God but not sure about Christ. This discovery became pivotal in presenting sermons like this one and in developing new Bible studies focused on pathways to discipleship. Even though the sermon is working with the results of the survey, notice how the figures in the painting provide a way of interpreting this study. Having experienced the painting, it now serves as a way of bringing our life experience into the scene depicted in the text and, more importantly, into relationship with Jesus.

About ten years ago, a study surveyed across the United States to discover any stages in spiritual growth as Christians. They found church members at four stages of growth, all of which are present in our church. Group One is comprised of church members still exploring the Christian faith. They believe in God, but they're not sure about Christ. That's right, some of us here, perhaps as many as 10 percent of us, are not yet confessing Christians. In Matthew language, we're not up from the table yet. Group Two is made up of those who are believers growing in Christ and getting to know him better. Still others of us in Group Three believe and are close to Christ, depending on him daily. And in Group Four are the most mature, the Christ-centered, who base every aspect of their life on him.

The same research discovered that those close to Christ can stall in that relationship. What's more, those centered in Christ can get frustrated that their church isn't going deep enough. Growth can stop, but it shouldn't. The Pharisees in Jesus's day got stopped in the mud of legalism, and Jesus told them that they were sick and needed healing. To be a Christian is to keep getting up and moving. It is changing, becoming more and more like the one we follow. It is knowing that without Jesus out front we are lost.

For us there is no greater reason to follow Jesus than the truth that he is worthy of being the one out front. He was out front to show us how to live and how to love. He was out front when he went the way of sorrows to the cross in our place. He was out front when he went headlong into death only to pioneer the way for us to resurrection and life. This is the Jesus we know. This is the Jesus we know, the Jesus we follow. He is worthy of our trust.

The sermon closes with a personal story which, frankly, I have told too often. Our favorite stories are often over-told. Its role as a parable next to the textual story will summarize and close the sermon, hopefully with a sigh that all is well and a final refrain of "Awesome!"

I will close with a story I love to tell from my time as a pastor in Oregon. I decided one fall to head up into the high Cascades to cut a noble fir tree for Christmas. Noble firs only grow at higher levels. I went up alone with a hand saw. Going up alone, I found out later, was not wise. I left in the afternoon, also unwise, I would learn. I stopped at the ranger station, got a permit for cutting the tree, and headed up to the mileage marker given me by the ranger. A pickup was parked near the marker. I parked there as well, and off I went into the woods.

Now I can be picky when it comes to Christmas trees, very picky. I spent hours looking for the perfect tree. I even went off trail, a bold move for a guy from Chicago. Snow began to fall softly at first and then heavily. I continued my quest for the perfect tree, forgetting that when snow falls, it cover's one's tracks. It was now getting late. I had no noble fir, and it was beginning to get dark. Worse, I discovered that I was lost, totally, utterly lost.

I managed to make it to a little opening in the woods where two trails met. Yes, it was a Robert Frost moment as "two roads diverged" in the woods. With panic setting in, I sat on a log and considered which road to take. (Years later, a student of mine would depict me there on that log facing two trails in the woods.) There on the log, I prayed for discernment. I looked to the left with hope. It was then I heard some rustling behind me. My first thought was that it had to be a bear. So this is the ending of my High Cascades adventure. I turned, and, amazing as it sounds, there approaching me was not a bear, but a member of our church, Jerry, dragging a perfect noble fir behind him. It was his pickup I had seen down at the mileage marker. He smiled, "Pastor Dean," he said, "you're lost, aren't you?"

"Totally, I said."

Then this man of the woods, who knew the mountains so well, put his hand on my shoulder and confidently said, "Follow me." I trusted him, so I followed him, on the trail to the right, not the left, all the way out of the woods. The next morning I found a perfect noble fir Christmas tree on our front porch.

This story has become a parable for me of the wonder of grace, the trust we can have in following Jesus, and the need to get up and move as a disciple. I have to tell that story to my new friend from the barbershop. I know exactly what he'll say when he hears it. Say it with me: "Awesome!" Amen.

Index of Art Citations

65 • Rembrandt van Rijn
Christ Preaching (La Petite Tombe), ca. 1652, Rijksmuseum, Amsterdam, The Netherlands

65 • Rembrandt van Rijn
Christ Preaching (The Hundred Guilder Print), 1646-1650, Rijksmuseum, Amsterdam, The Netherlands

50 • Rembrandt van Rijn
Christ in the Storm on the Lake of Galilee, 1633, Isabella Stewart Gardner Museum, Boston, Massachusetts (Stolen 1990)

70, 71 • Rembrandt van Rijn
The Return of the Prodigal Son, 1669, Hermitage Museum, St. Petersburg, Russia

128 • Rembrandt van Rijn,
Simeon's Song of Praise, 1631, The Mauritshuis, The Hague, The Netherlands

130 • Rembrandt van Rijn,
Simeon's Song of Praise, 1669, Nationalmuseum, Stockholm, Sweden

108 • Francisco Ribalta
The Crucifixion or Saint Francis Embracing the Crucified Christ, ca. 1620, Museo de Bellas Artes de Valencia, Spain

112 • Georges Rouault
Crucifixion, 1937, Minneapolis Institute of Art, Minneapolis, Minnesota

35, 36 • Andrei Rublev
The Trinity, 1425-1427, Tretyakov Gallery, Moscow, Russia

80 • Bertel Thorvaldsen
Christus (Sculpture), 1829, Church of Our Lady Copenhagen. Denmark

113 • Titian
Noli Me Tangere (Do Not Touch Me), ca. 1514, The National Gallery, London, England

98 • Unknown
The Alexamenos Graffito, 3rd century, Palatine Hill, Rome, Italy

100 • Unknown
Christ as Emperor, 4th century, Santa Pudenziana Church, Rome, Italy

98, 99 • Unknown
Christ the Good Shepherd, 3rd century, Catacomb of Callistus, Rome, Italy

100 • Unknown
Christ as Warrior King, After 500 AD, Museo Arcivescovile, Ravenna, Italy

100 • Unknown
Christ with Beard, 4th century, Catacomb of Commodilla, Rome, Italy

100, 101 • Unknown
Christ Pantocrator, 6th century, Monastery of St. Catherine, Egypt

103 • Unknown
The Crucifixion of Christ, 420-430 AD, British Museum, London, England

99 • Unknown
Healing of the Paralytic, 3rd century, Dura Europos Collection, Yale University Gallery of Fine Arts, New Haven, Connecticut

99 • Unknown
The Raising of Lazarus, 3rd century, Catacomb of Callistus, Rome, Italy

103 • Unknown
The Road to Calvary, 6th century, Basilica of Sant' Apollinare Nuova. Ravenna, Italy

110 • Diego Velázquez
Christ Crucified, 1632, Museo del Prado, Madrid, Spain

77 • Egbert van der Poel
A View of Delft After the Explosion of 1654, 1654, The National Gallery, London, England

75, 76 • Vincent van Gogh
The Raising of Lazarus (after Rembrandt), 1890, Van Gogh Museum, Amsterdam, The Netherlands

50 • Johannes Vermeer
Jesus in the House of Mary and Martha, 1654-1656, National Galleries of Scotland, Edinburgh, Scotland

67, 68 • George Frederick Watts
Hope, 1885, Watts Gallery, London, England